DEPARTMENT OF HEALTH

The Children Act 1989 Guidance and Regulations

Volume 8

Private Fostering and Miscellaneous

A NEW FRAMEWORK FOR THE CARE
AND UPBRINGING OF CHILDREN

LONDON: HMSO

© Crown copyright 1991
First published 1991
ISBN 0 11 321473 1

Preface

This volume is number eight in a series produced in the context of the Children Act 1989 and issued under section 7 of the Local Authority Social Services Act 1970. It contains guidance and regulations on four separate subjects under the following headings:-

Chapter 1:   Services for Children Fostered by Private Arrangements

Chapter 2:   Disqualification for Caring for Children

Chapter 3:   Childminding and Day Care: Regulations on Applications for Registration and Registration and Inspection Fees

Chapter 4:   Arrangements to Assist Children to Live Abroad.

Local authorities will need to review their existing policies and practice in the light of the regulations and guidance and give the same priority to these responsibilities as to other statutory duties.

For a proper understanding of other relevant guidance and regulations, Chapter 1 should be read in conjunction with other volumes in the series, particularly Volume 3: 'Family Placements'. Chapter 3 should be read in conjunction with Volume 2: 'Family Support, Day Care and Educational Provision for Young People'.

Regulations and guidance associated with Chapter 2 of this volume applies to private fostering, childminding, day care and residential care.

Regulations associated with the guidance in this volume are contained in the annex.

The Department wishes to acknowledge the work of Barbara Lerner and Laurie Joshua in the preparation of Chapter 1.

Contents

ANNEXES — 41

CHAPTER 1 SERVICES FOR CHILDREN FOSTERED BY PRIVATE ARRANGEMENTS

PART 1.1 INTRODUCTION

1.1.1. The Children Act 1989 brings together in a single coherent legislative framework private and public law relating to children. It aims to strike a balance between the rights of parents to exercise their responsibilities towards the child, the rights of children to express their views on decisions made about their lives and the duty of the state to intervene where a child's welfare requires it.

1.1.2. This first chapter of Volume 8 is about private fostering arrangements and the regulatory, supervisory and advisory roles of local authorities. The relevant legislation is set out in Part IX of the Act, in Schedules 7 & 8 and in section 24 of the Act (after care). Regulations made under Part IX of the Act are included in the Annex A to this volume.

1.1.3. The Children (Private Arrangements for Fostering) Regulations 1991 exercise the powers contained in section 67(2) and paragraph 7 of Schedule 8 by requiring that local authorities satisfy themselves about certain matters regarding the welfare of privately fostered children (Regulation 2), that authorities are to visit privately fostered children on specified occasions (Regulation 3), about notifications by prospective and actual foster parents to local authorities (Regulation 4), by former foster parents (Regulation 5), other notifications (Regulation 5) and the form of notifications (Regulation 7).

1.1.4. The Children Act provisions supercede those contained in the Foster Children Act 1980. These new Regulations include visits to children. There are a number of other changes, including the definition of private fostering.

1.1.5. Referring to the welfare of privately fostered children, the 1989 Act states that "It shall be the duty of every local authority to satisfy themselves that the welfare of children who are privately fostered in their area is being satisfactorily safeguarded and promoted and to secure that such advice is given to those caring for them as appears to the authority to be needed" [section 67(1)]. Private fostering is the arrangement made between usually the parent and the private foster parent, who becomes responsible for caring for the child in such a way as to promote and safeguard his welfare. The role of local authorities is to satisfy themselves that the arrangements are satisfactory and that the foster parents are suitable. *They do not approve or register private foster parents*. A proper balance, therefore, needs to be maintained between parental private responsibilities and statutory duties towards private foster children.

1.1.6. The attention of local authority social services is drawn to the publication: 'The Care of Children: Principles and Practice in Regulations and Guidance' which was first produced by the Department of Health in 1989. This publication will assist practitioners and supervisors to relate law to practice and to understand the context in which regulations and guidance are issued.

1.1.7. The term 'foster parent' is used throughout the text of this document since the term is well understood by the general public and is the preferred term in Regulations made under the Act. We recognise, however, that the term 'foster carer' is now more commonly used among professionals.

1.2.1 Part IX of the Children Act contains provisions relating to private arrangements for fostering children. Section 66 provides the definitions:

'(1)(a) "a privately fostered child" means a child who is under the age of sixteen and who is cared for, and provided with accommodation by, someone other than -

    (i) a parent of his;

    (ii) a person who is not a parent of his but who has parental responsibility for him; or

    (iii) a relative of his; and

(b) "to foster a child privately" means to look after the child in circumstances in which he is a privately fostered child as defined by this section.

(2) A child is not a privately fostered child if the person caring for and accommodating him —

(a) has done so for a period of less than 28 days; and

(b) does not intend to do so for any longer period.

(3) Subsection (1) is subject to —

(a) the provisions of section 63; and

(b) the exceptions made by paragraphs 1 to 5 of Schedule 8.

(4) In the case of a child who is disabled, subsection (1) (a) shall have effect as if for "sixteen" there were substituted "eighteen".

Schedule 8 to the Act sets out the exemptions to the definition as in paragraphs 1-2:

"1. A child is not a privately fostered child while he is being looked after by a local authority.

1.2.2. (1) A child is not a privately fostered child while he is in the care of any person —

(a) in premises in which any —

    (i) parent of his;

    (ii) person who is not a parent of his but who has parental responsibility for him; or

    (iii) person who is a relative of his and who has assumed responsibility for his care,

is for the time being living:

(b) in any children's home;

(c) in accommodation provided by or on behalf of any voluntary organisation;

(d) in any school in which he is receiving full-time education;

(e) in any health service hospital;

(f) in any residential care home, nursing home or mental nursing home; or

(g) in any home or institution not specified in this paragraph but provided, equipped and maintained by the Secretary of State.

(2) Sub-paragraph (1)(b) to (g) does not apply where the person caring for the child is doing so in his personal capacity and not in the course of carrying out his duties in relation to the establishment mentioned in the paragraph in question.

1.2.3. A child is not a privately fostered child while is in the care of any person in compliance with —

1969 c.54 (a) an order under section 7(7)(b) of the Children and Young Persons Act 1969; or

1968 c.49 (b) a supervision requirement within the meaning of the Social Work (Scotland) Act 1968.

1.2.4. A child is not a privately fostered child while he is liable to be detained, or subject to guardianship, under the Mental Health Act 1983.

1.2.5. A child is not a private fostered child while —

(a) he is placed in the care of a person who proposes to adopt him under arrangements made by an adoption agency within the meaning of —

1976 c.36 (i) section 1 of the Adoption Act 1976;

1978 c.28 (ii) section 1 of the Adoption (Scotland) Act 1978; or

SI 1987/2203 (iii) Article 3 of the Adoption (Northern Ireland) Order 1987; or

(b) he is a protected child within the meaning of section 32 of the Adoption Act 1976.

1.2.6. The welfare of privately fostered children is addressed in section 67. Subsection (2) of section 67 empowers the Secretary of State to regulate how local authorities carry out their duties to privately fostered children while paragraph 7 of Schedule 8 provides for regulations requiring notification of a child who is or is proposed to be fostered privately. Paragraph 6 of Schedule 8 provides local authorities with powers to impose requirements in carrying out their duty under section 67. The local authority can impose requirements on the person who is or intends to privately foster a child as to:

(a) the number, age and sex of the children who may be privately fostered by him;

(b) the standard of accommodation and equipment to be provided for them;

(c) the arrangements to be made with respect to their health and safety; and

(d) particular arrangements which must be made with respect to the provision of care for them, and it shall be his duty to comply with any such requirement before the end of such period as the authority may specify unless, in the case of a proposal, the proposal is not carried out".

1.2.7. Paragraph 6 provides that any requirement should be notified in writing with reasons and that the notification should inform the person of his right to appeal (contained in paragraph 8 of the Schedule) and the time limit for doing so.

1.2.8. Section 68 of the Act deals with disqualification from being a private foster parent and provides for Regulations which set out the circumstances in which this may occur and the notices that should be given. The Regulations — The Disqualification for Caring for Children Regulations 1991 — are included in Annex B to this volume. A power to prohibit private fostering is contained in section 69; section 70 sets out details of the offence committed if requirements of the Act and Regulations are not met. Details concerning offences under the Act relating to private fostering are given in paragraphs 1.8.30.–1.8.33.

PART 1.3: STATUTORY REQUIREMENTS: SUMMARY

Notification

1.3.1. A proposal to foster a child privately must be notified to the local authority in whose area the fostering will take place. The detailed requirements of notification are set down in the Regulations. Notification has to be given by the prospective foster parent and any other person who is involved in the arrangement. A parent of the child who is to be privately fostered must also notify the local authority if he knows of the arrangement even if he is not involved directly in making the arrangements.

Welfare of the Child

1.3.2. Responsibility for safeguarding and promoting the welfare of the private foster child rests with the parent. Local authorities are required to satisfy themselves that the welfare of privately fostered children in their area is satisfactorily safeguarded and promoted. They must also ensure that private foster parents are given advice, where it appears to the authority to be needed [section 67(1)]. The Regulations set out the circumstances in which local authorities should visit private foster children and how local authorities should carry out their functions in respect of these children.

Premises

1.3.3. The authority may inspect premises in which private fostering is taking place, or is proposed to take place, and may also enquire about and interview the children in them [section 67(3)]. Requirements may be imposed by the local authority on private foster parents, such as the number of children who may be accommodated and the arrangements which must be made for their care [Schedule 7, paragraphs 2 and 4 and Schedule 8, paragraph 6].

Prohibitions and Requirements

1.3.4. Prohibitions may be imposed by the local authority if a person is not suitable to foster a child, the premises are not suitable for fostering or it would be prejudicial to the welfare of the child for him to be or continue to be fostered by the person in the premises concerned [section 69(1)–(3)]. Regulations also specify the circumstances in which a person is disqualified from privately fostering a child without the consent of the local authority [section 68].

1.3.5. If local authorities are not satisfied about the welfare of children privately fostered, they should inform the parents or those having parental responsibility for the child. They must also consider whether they should exercise any of their functions under the Act [section 67(5)]. An authority may decide to impose requirements or even a prohibition on the foster parent; the duty to investigate under Part V of the Act may be necessary. If the local authority need to remove the child, they may consider applying for an emergency protection order or a care order, Unless it would not be in the best interests of the child concerned, they must take reasonable steps to secure that the child is looked after by a parent or relative of his or someone else who exercises parental responsibility for him [section 67(5)].

1.3.6. Where the local authority make a decision about a requirement, prohibition or a disqualified person, an appeal may be made to the court within 14 days of notification of that decision [Schedule 8, paragraph 8]. An offence may be committed if there is a failure to notify the local authority of private fostering arrangements, breaches of requirement, prohibitions `and disqualifications, and obstruction of powers of entry [section 70]. An application for a search warrant under section 102 of the Act may be necessary to support the power of entry.

In Need

1.3.7. Section 17(10), Part III of the Act gives local authorities a general duty to safeguard and promote the welfare of children in need and to promote the upbringing of such children by their families, so far as this is consistent with the welfare duty to the child. The definition of 'need' in the Act is deliberately wide to reinforce the emphasis on preventative support and services. It has three categories:

(i) reasonable standard of health (physical or mental health) or development;

(ii) significant impairment of health or development; and

(iii) disablement.

1.3.8. It would not be acceptable for a local authority to exempt any of these three categories from consideration where the children in question are being, or are proposed to be, privately fostered, or by confining services to children at risk of significant harm which attracts the duty to investigate under section 47. The child's needs which are to be considered also include physical, emotional and educational needs according to his age, gender, race, religion, culture and language. The capacity of the proposed or current private foster parent to meet those needs must also be considered. (See Part 5: Suitability of the Foster Parent).

1.3.9. This guidance does not lay down firm criteria or set general priorities because the Act requires each authority to decide its own level and scale of services appropriate to children in need in their area. However, because the definition is in the Act, a local authority cannot lawfully substitute any other definition for the purposes of Part III. It may be that a parent, or person with parental responsibility for a child, who proposes to have him privately fostered could be provided with services under section 17(3) of the Act to safeguard the welfare of the child and to enable the parent, or person with parental responsibility, to continue to look after him. The outcome of any service provision under this power should be evaluated to see whether it has met the primary objective of safeguarding and promoting the child's welfare.

Meeting Needs

1.3.10. Section 17 and Part 1 of Schedule 2 to the Act set out the specific duties and powers of local authorities in relation to support services for children with families. Under section 17(1) local authorities have a general duty to provide a range and level of services appropriate to the children in their area who are 'in need' so as to safeguard and promote their welfare and, so far as is consistent with that aim, promote their upbringing by their families. Local authorities are not expected to meet every individual need, but they are asked to identify the extent of need and then make decisions on the priorities for service provision in their area in the light of that information and their statutory duties. Local authorities will have to ensure that a range of services is available to meet the extent and nature of need identified within their administrative areas.

Limit on the Number of Foster Children

1.3.11. The provisions of Schedule 7 of the Act prescribe the usual fostering limit of not more than three children. This provision includes a foster parent who fosters a child by private arrangement. More detailed guidance on the number of children in foster homes and exemptions to the provision is contained in Volume 3 'Family Placements', page 34–35.

PART 1.4: ARRANGING THE PLACEMENT OF CHILDREN

Parental Responsibility

1.4.1. Parental responsibility is one of the key provisions of the Act. Because parents carry the prime responsibility they should be encouraged to participate in (and mainly initiate) all the decision making processes in the placement. It is most important for the well being of the child that the parent provides the prospective foster parent with as much information about the child as possible, including health record, diet preferences, school records, hobbies, religion, ethnicity etc.

1.4.2. The Act defines 'parental responsibility' to include all the rights, powers and duties of parents in relation to a child and his property, [section 3(1)].

1.4.3. A person, such as a private foster parent, who has care (ie 'actual custody') of a child for whom he does not have parental responsibility is empowered [section 3(5)] to do what is reasonable in all circumstances to safeguard and promote the welfare of the child. A person with parental responsibility, such as the parent of a child, may arrange under section 2(9) for the private foster parent to meet that responsibility, by delegating responsibility, for example, for consent to medical treatment. Such an arrangement may prove useful in situations where the parent of the child is unable to exercise his responsibilities. However, under section 2(11), such an arrangement does not affect any liability of the person with parental responsibility which may follow from a failure to meet that responsibility.

1.4.4. People other than parents, such as a private foster parent, who do not have parental responsibility for a particular child, may acquire parental responsibility by being appointed guardian or by an order of the court (a residence order or by adoption). Section 5 of the Act covers the appointment of a guardian and Schedules 10 and 15 of the Act relate to changes in Adoption.

1.4.5. There is a basic principle throughout the Act that parents retain their responsibilities and shall remain as closely involved as is consistent with their child's welfare, particularly if the child has special health and development needs.

1.4.6. Whilst the day to day care of the child can be delegated to the private foster parent, parental responsibility is retained by the natural parent. How they exercise this is also a matter for agreement with the private foster parent. Although it may suit the natural and foster parents that the former fades from the child's life leaving a quasi adoption situation, this drift could leave the position of the child insecure. Frank discussion is important between all parties including the child, if practicable. If plans change, the reasons given for the change and the nature of the revised arrangements should be clearly understood by all parties, including the child. Foster care however, should never be regarded as a 'back door' to adoption.

1.4.7. If the natural parents are falling short of their responsibilities, eg failing to pay maintenance or to keep in touch, the social worker should try to locate the mother and find out if there is a problem, give advice and take appropriate action as necessary.

Purpose and Duration of Arrangement

1.4.8. The purpose and intended duration of a fostering arrangement needs to be clearly established by the local authority prior to the placement and details should be included on the notification, It should be reviewed on every visit so that any change can be anticipated to enable parent, child and other carers to be involved and consulted, thus helping to avoid unplanned moves or drift. Where it is likely that any difficulties will be resolved by the child being moved precipitately, a requirement that the local authority should be informed in advance should be considered so that action discussed below in "Continuity and Change" (1.7.28) and "Unsatisfactory Care" (1.8.13) can be explored.

Child Development

1.4.9. The child's physical, intellectual, emotional, social and behavioural development would be expected to include appropriate and sufficient diet, exercise, play, intellectual stimulation, identification of disabilities, help (where necessary) with language development, child's identity and self esteem, relationships, social skills and behaviour, ensuring that his needs are appropriately assessed and satisfactorily met and his views heard.

Well Being

1.4.10. Emotional well-being is made up of a number of factors, including,

(a) the quality and permanence of previous care and relationships;

(b) how separation and loss are being handled. (Both parents and private foster parents may need advice.);

(c) the amount of continuity in his life, ie whether only part of his life has changed or his total environment. (The passing on of information about likes, habits, experiences and history is important here, see paragraphs 1.7.28–1.7.33.)

(d) his sense of self worth which comes from being loved, respected and accepted as an individual in his own right, and a sense of belonging to his new family and social setting and not being discriminated against;

(e) his self image and sense of identity, including ethnicity, knowing who his parents are and having a consistent name. (It is important that natural parents inform the new carers how he is normally addressed.) Foster parents should not attempt to 'anglicise' the name of a child from an ethnic minority family. The parents should be encouraged to leave photos of themselves and family and keep the child up to date with happenings in the family and also impart background information to the child direct and or through the foster parents. The foster parent should encourage this as well as contact with any siblings also fostered, the natural family and significant people from the past.

1.4.11. Disturbed behaviour may be a reflection of emotional difficulties which in turn may be related to past or present experiences. It is an indication that all is not well and an assessment of the problems is needed so that appropriate advice can be given and if necessary, action taken. The happiness of the child, quality and comfort of relationships, whether he is insecure or confused, are also indicators of emotional state as is as the reaction and attitudes of the foster family to the foster child and his needs.

1.4.12. As much information as possible about the child and his needs should be shared by the parents with the prospective carers before placement so that they can measure the task they propose to take on.

1.4.13. Advice can be given on appropriate play, nursery school or playgroup experience, leisure activities and experiences that will enhance his feeling of self worth and identify and stimulate his intellect.

1.4.14. If the child has special needs, or is "in need" within the definition of the Act, he should receive the appropriate services ranging from sponsorship to a playgroup, to services for children who are disabled and their carers. Further guidance on services to be provided for children in need and those with disabilities is contained in Volume 2 which contains guidance and Regulations relating to family support, day care and educational provision for young children.

Religion, Culture, Language and Race

1.4.15. Regulation 2(2)(c) makes specific reference to the needs of the child arising from religion, culture, language and race and the local authority's duty to satisfy themselves that these needs are being met by the particular arrangements made for fostering the child. These issues are discussed more fully in paragraphs 1.7.21–1.7.24.

Financial Arrangements

1.4.16. Prospective foster parents should have realistic expectations about costs to adequately maintain a child. They should also be clear about how far they are prepared to contribute to the child's maintenance (if at all). In any event they should have sufficient resources to tide over any gaps in maintenance payments, at least temporarily, to give time for plans to be made without the child being summarily moved. Exceptionally, action by the local authority could be considered to assist the foster family through a short period of financial hardship which was simultaneous with a fall in maintenance payments. Such payments can be recovered. Any state entitlements should also be taken into account.

1.4.17. Private foster parents can receive child benefit (see Department of Social Security leaflet CH4) but any maintenance payments received will be counted as full maintenance in any assessment for Social Security benefits.

Suitability of Accommodation

1.4.18. Section 67(3) requires the local authority to inspect the premises where a privately fostered child is being, or is proposed to be, accommodated and to satisfy itself about the suitability of the accommodation. The type of accommodation used to privately foster a child will vary considerably and local authorities should decide whether the standard of a particular accommodation satisfies criteria for suitability, having regard to the child's age and welfare.

1.4.19. The local authority should refer to Volume 2, paragraph 7.33(a), as well as the following points, when deciding on the suitability of accommodation:

- safety of fires, electrical sockets, windows, floor coverings and glass doors;
- cooking facilities and safety in the kitchen or cooking area;
- equipment, such as cots, should be British Standard approved;
- use of stairgates;
- safe storage of medicines and dangerous household substances;
- presence of pets and arrangements for their control;
- quality of transport — car seats, safety belts, etc;
- washing and toilet facilities;
- outside playspace;
- fire safety, eg smoke detectors and matches stored in a secure place;
- access to garden and safety within it and access to the road.

1.4.20. When inspecting premises where a privately fostered child is being accommodated, the local authority should take into account such conditions as dampness and extremes of temperature which will have a direct effect on the health of a child who has conditions such as sickle cell anaemia or thalassaemia.

Those proposing to privately foster a child should be made aware of the factors being considered when assessment of the accommodation is made.

1.4.21. The assessment should also include living and sleeping facilities and the effect of possible overcrowding. Where a child is to share a bedroom with another member of the household, particular attention should be give to ensuring that the arrangements will not be prejudicial to his welfare. It is important for a child to have his own bed. Under normal circumstances a private foster child, over the age of two, should not share a bedroom with a teenager, the foster parent or other adult member of the household.

Health Care

1.4.22. Health care should be an essential part of a parent's responsibility in safeguarding and promoting the welfare of the child. Children of certain racial origins or from certain parts of the world may have particular health care needs and full consideration should be given to this aspect of the child's care. If a child is well and active then no special screening may need to be undertaken, over and above routine screening and surveillance offered to all children in the United Kingdom. If, however, the child is unwell, special factors should be taken into account as they may be the key to the child's ill health. For example, children of particular racial origins or from certain parts of the world may be at risk from sickle cell disease, thalassaemia, tuberculosis, hepatitis B, or tropical diseases such as malaria.

1.4.23. Children with disabilities may have been receiving medical services from specialist units and special arrangements may be necessary to ensure continuity of care and treatment [Regulation 2(2)(b)]. If the parents hold the personal child health record (PCHR) this should be handed to the foster parent, (see also paragraphs 1.7.5–1.7.8). Local authorities should enquire whether health authorities and Family Health Service Authorities are aware of the arrangements to ensure continuity. The parents of the child to be privately fostered should make known the child's medical history to the prospective foster parents and the local authority.

Education

1.4.24. For school-age children, remaining at the same school offers not only continuity of education but also continuity in an important part of the child's daily life. The level of disruption caused by any proposed, or actual, change in schools will have to be carefully considered by the social worker.

1.4.25. Regulation 2(2)(g) places an obligation on local authorities to satisfy themselves about arrangements for the child's education and that the local education authority has been informed of the fostering arrangements.

Physical Care

1.4.26. Expectations regarding the physical care of the child should be established from the first contact between parents and foster parents and are best achieved through co-operation, encouragement, availability of advice and mediation, all of which focus on achieving the best interests of the child.

1.4.27. Help and advice should be made available to private foster parents on all aspects of child care including the numbers, ages and sex of the children fostered. Requirements can be made and advice given regarding safety and equipment, eg. British Standard cots and pushchairs. If the overall standard of care remains unsatisfactory then appropriate action, involving the natural parents, should be taken.

Further Enquiries

1.4.28. As well as the initial assessment including the taking up of personal references, the suitability of a foster parent needs to be monitored at intervals. A visit may be needed upon notification of a change in the household, conviction or other circumstance. At each visit enquiries should be made about any changes as the requirement to notify may have been overlooked by the foster parent. Regulation 3 places a duty on the officer making a visit to provide the local authority with a written report.

1.4.29. The quality of the relationship between the child and his foster family is a useful barometer as to suitability as well as all the matters detailed in this section on the Regulations.

Advice to the Foster Parent

1.4.30. Regulations place a duty on the local authority to satisfy themselves on a number of issues, including whether the foster parent is being given any necessary advice, Regulation 2(2)(j).

1.4.31. If the foster parent is not receiving necessary advice, the social worker should help to secure it. "Necessary" advice pertains to all matters detailed under the Act, Schedules 7 & 8 and the Regulations. The advice should also include the wider implications of fostering such as racial harassment. Foster parents need to be prepared for it and to deal with it.

1.4.32. Advice might also include the desirability of taking out public liability insurance cover. If foster parents carry household insurance they should inform the insurance company that the household includes foster children.

1.4.33. Advice to foster parents can be given in a number of ways:

- individually by the social worker, health visitor or other professional;

- in a "self-help" group, learning from other foster parents. This can be particularly useful if it includes some experienced foster parents with good standards of care who can act as role models to others;

- via "Drop in" centres, possibly with child minders;

- by being linked to the provision of resources, eg a toy library or equipment loan scheme, or alongside a play group;

- training set up specifically for private foster parents or generally for all foster parents, childminders or others.

Contact with the Child's Family

1.4.34. Where the placement will not be, or is not, within easy reach of the child's family, the local authority should explore whether firm arrangements can be made to facilitate contact. Contacts with members of the child's extended family who are living in the UK should also be encouraged. Where the proposed or actual private foster parent is from a different racial or cultural group to that of the child, the local authority should make the foster parents aware of the need to make provisions that would enable close links to be maintained with the child's cultural heritage, [Regulation 2(2)(c) and (k)].

1.4.35. The need for contact with significant people in the child's earlier life should be thoroughly explored at the initial enquiry stage. Natural and foster parents may need advice on the importance of continuing links for the child's emotional welfare.

1.4.36. Arrangements for contact with the natural parent need to be clear and honoured so that the child knows where he stands and is reassured that his family still care. Equally, arrangements for contact with siblings, relatives, persons with parental responsibilities and others should be organised and the arrangements set down in writing. Arrangements for the foster parent to contact the natural parent should also be set down. If the adult carers are working together then the child is more likely to feel secure.

1.4.37. At every visit the social worker should enquire about the existing arrangements and, if appropriate, offer advice and help in resolving any difficulty, even, if necessary, a venue for families to meet. Normally the financial costs are a matter between the natural and foster parents but financial assistance could be considered under section 17 of the Act if this supports a child in "need" as defined by the Act. (See paragraph 1.8.14).

1.4.38. Natural parents may need to be advised on the desirability to keep siblings together if possible-unless a child has particular needs which have to be met separately. In any event the arrangements between parents and foster parents should ensure that contact between siblings is maintained where possible.

Wishes of the Child

1.4.39. The child's views should always be sought, subject to the child's ability to understand. This may create anxiety in the foster parent and time may be needed to deal with this. Also, the social worker should be clear on how confidences should be handled. The child's views on his becoming, or actually being, a privately fostered child needs to be taken into account when placement is being considered. The social worker should be particularly aware that there may be good reasons why the child's views are different from those of his parents, or any other person with parental responsibility for him and, in the case of a child who is privately fostered, the views of the private foster parent. The more mature the child, the more fully he will be able to enter into discussion about plans and proposals and participate in the decision-making process. With young children too, the social worker should make efforts to discover their true feelings.

1.4.40. The social worker should take all reasonable steps to ensure that the principle of partnership with the child's parents and foster parents is maintained at all stages of the consultations. All children need to be given information and explanations so that they are in a position to develop their own views and make choices. Providing children with reassurance and helping them over their anxieties is essential if their welfare is to be safeguarded and promoted. If this is sensitively handled, children will not be made to feel that the burden of decision making falls totally upon them.

1.4.41. Where the child has communication difficulties, social workers need to ensure that all necessary means are employed to enable the child to express his views, feelings and consent (or not) and for those views to be considered. Such means could include consulting someone who has the appropriate communication skills such as sign language and making use of Makaton or Bliss symbols — a language of signs used by people with severe learning difficulties. With very young children their wishes and feelings can often be established indirectly by observation and through play or, in the case of a very disturbed child, through any therapy which the child may be receiving.

1.4.42. In the case of a child whose first language is not English, an interpreter may be required. The importance to a child of maintaining his first language should be addressed since eventual return to his family or community is made even more difficult if he is unable to use his "own" language.

PART 1.5: SUITABILITY OF THE FOSTER PARENT

Enquiries

1.5.1. Enquiries are to be conducted by the local authority for the purpose of determining the suitability of persons who proposes to foster a child privately, or is privately fostering a child whom he is already caring for and providing accommodation. The enquiries must always be linked to the duty of the local authority to satisfy itself that the welfare of the child is being satisfactorily safeguarded and promoted while privately fostered [section 67(1)].
Determining the suitability of the person and his accommodation and ensuring that the arrangements are satisfactorily promoting and safeguarding the child's welfare can best be accomplished by:

● consulting the person who proposes to foster a child and the parent (or person with parental responsibility) about the reasons to have him privately fostered;

● making advice available to the person who is to fostering a child privately.

1.5.2. Discussions with the person who is fostering a child privately should be frank. It should always be made clear by the social worker that the welfare of the child is paramount. The enquiry process should provide opportunities to enable a prospective foster parent to opt out of the proposed arrangements. The person who is fostering or proposing to foster a child privately should be given a clear understanding as to the purpose of the enquiries so that they fully comprehend the duty of the social worker to determine:

a) the suitability of the person and his household;

b) the suitability of the accommodation in which the child is to be privately fostered;

c) that neither would be prejudicial to the welfare of the child, and

d) that arrangements or the proposed arrangements are likely to provide a safe and stable environment for the child.

Local authority enquiries into establishing suitability of the foster parent can take place before a placement or after a placement has begun and should take particular account of the following aspects:

Police Records

1.5.3. Persons proposing to foster a child privately should provide written consent for police records to be checked for previous convictions, (see Annex A). Authorities should check their own records of the person and other members of the household and liaise with other local authorities if the proposed foster parent has only been in the present local authority area for a short-time. A record of convictions will not necessarily preclude the person from fostering a child privately, but will require careful consideration in consultation with senior staff. The disqualification provisions contained in section 68 of the Act and the Disqualification for Caring for Children Regulations are relevant in this respect.

1.5.4. The Police should also be asked to check the records of all members of the household. Unless members of the household agree to police checks being made local authorities will not be able to satisfy themselves as to the welfare of the child. Authorities should note that exceptions to the Rehabilitation of Offenders Act orders `would apply to these checks.

Household Relationships

1.5.5. Social workers should visit on at least one occasion to meet the entire household. The extent to which other members of the household may participate in the daily care of a privately fostered child is an important consideration, as are demands made by other members of the household on the foster parent or prospective foster parent. The impact of fostering a child privately on family life should be discussed fully with that person and the whole family. The extent of contact with persons staying with the family should also be explored. Where the person is over 16 and the degree of contact and involvement is significant, the guidance in paragraph 1.5.3 above may be relevant.

Parenting Capacity

1.5.6. The social worker should form a view on the parenting capacity of the person proposing to foster a child privately and should consult with appropriate agencies. The health visitor may, for example, be able to provide insights into the person's experience of caring for children of different age groups, children of a particular ethnic minority group, children with special needs or caring for children in general. The person proposing to foster a child should be made aware that such views will be sought.

Religion

1.5.7. Attention may need to be given to the expectations of the private foster child participating in the religious life of the person and his household and whether this would be compatible with the expectations of a child and his parents.

Ethnicity

1.5.8. In circumstances where it is known that a child comes from an minority ethnic group or from a particular cultural background, the social worker should seek to establish whether the person proposing to foster the child has an understanding of the particular culture and knowledge of the child's language. (see guidance on race, culture, religion and linguistic needs, paragraphs 1.7.21–1.7.24) Social workers should explore the extent to which the prospective foster parent is prepared to develop such understanding and give advice as appropriate. (Section 71 of the Race Relations Act 1976 places a duty on local authorities to eliminate racial discrimination).

Parental Visits

1.5.9. The foster parent's or prospective foster parent's attitudes and expectations should be explored concerning his promoting contact between the child's parent, or person with parental responsibility, and his willingness to facilitate visits by parents and relatives to the foster home for the duration of the placement. It is essential that the person fostering or proposing to foster a child is aware of the implications of caring for other people's children and of the need to work in partnership with the child's parent.

Life Style

1.5.10. The social worker will need to determine the standard of living and "life style" of the person and, for example, should explore the type of leisure activities and other interests pursued and how the type of employment affects family life. Where the person fostering or proposing to foster a child is employed outside the home, arrangements should be made by the foster parent to ensure proper care for the child after school and during sickness and holidays. Account should also be taken of the foster parent's willingness to provide a child from an ethnic minority community with a diet which is familiar to him, including food which may be part of a religious observance.

Education

1.5.11. The social worker should explore the foster parent's or prospective foster parent's attitudes and expectations in relation to a child's education. The objective should be to establish a view as to the person's:

- understanding and recognition of the need to provide educational support to a privately fostered child, including a commitment to ensure the child's regular attendance at school;
- ability to cope with the challenge in providing support to a child with special educational needs.

1.5.12. The Social Worker should discuss these issues with the foster parent and provide information whenever appropriate about the range of statutory and voluntary agencies which can offer support.

Discipline

1.5.13. The social worker should explore the foster parent's views on discipline, including a preparedness to accept that corporal punishment is inappropriate for children who are privately fostered. The term "corporal punishment" should be taken to cover any intentional application of force as a form of punishment, including slapping, pinching, squeezing, shaking, throwing objects and rough handling. It would also include punching or pushing in the heat of the moment in response to violence from young people. It does not prevent a person taking necessary physical action where any other course of action would be unlikely to avert immediate danger of personal injury to the child or to another person, or to avoid immediate danger to property. Verbal abuse, derogatory remarks and pointed jokes can cause psychological harm to the child.

1.5.14. It would be quite inappropriate for a child to be refused meals. The enjoyment derived from eating and drinking is well established and it is fundamental to a child's physical and emotional development. Meal times are also an important social occasion in the life of a child. Deprivation of food and drink should be interpreted to include the denial of access to the amounts and range of food and drink normally available to children in the home, (but would not include instances where specific food or drinks have to be withheld from a child on medical advice).

Similarly, restriction of visits to and from the family and friends of a child who is privately fostered should not be used as punishment.

(The National Foster Care Association has produced a useful booklet on the subject of discipline, entitled 'Managing Behaviour').

I Notifications by prospective and actual foster parents

Timescale

1.6.1. Except in an emergency, a person who proposes to foster a child by private arrangement and is not yet providing accommodation for that child is required to notify the local authority not less than 6 weeks and not more than 13 weeks before he receives the child.

1.6.2. The requirement in Regulation 4(2) is that any person receiving a child in an emergency or already caring for and providing accommodation for a child, when he became a 'privately fostered child', must notify the local authority for the area in which the child is privately fostered, and should do so not more than 48 hours after the fostering arrangement begins. This notice must be given in writing. This requirement will often apply where the person was registered as a child minder, for a particular child aged under 8 for the first 28 days of placement, immediately after that 28 days has expired.

Emergencies

1.6.3 In some cases, such as in an emergency or where the child is already being privately fostered, it may not be possible to carry out extensive enquiries immediately. However, clear procedures should be drawn up for undertaking enquiries for children who are notified to the local authority in an emergency, or after the child is found in situ. A plan for conducting such enquiries should be implemented without undue delay. Once this process has been initiated, the parent, or person with parental responsibility for the child, should be informed and appropriate notification forms sent.

Content of Notice

1.6.4. The specific details required by local authorities which constitute a notification to foster a child is contained in Regulation 4(3).

Disqualification

1.6.5. Under Section 68 certain people are disqualified from privately fostering children. Local authorities will need to conduct appropriate enquiries to determine whether a proposed, or actual, foster parent is disqualified from private fostering, or whether any member of the persons household is disqualified from fostering a child privately. The legal department will need to be consulted to establish procedures when a person is found to be disqualified and on the procedures for handling appeals by a disqualified person as provided by Schedule 8, paragraph 8(c).

1.6.6. As an effective and efficient means of establishing whether or not a person is disqualified from fostering privately, local authorities may consider using a declaration form as shown in Annex A, and enable the person to give their written consent for enquiries to be made with other agencies.

1.6.7. Local authorities can, in certain circumstances, give their consent to a person acting as a private foster parent who would otherwise be disqualified, but only if they are satisfied that a child's welfare would not be prejudiced by the foster parent or prospective foster parent or by a member of that parent's household. In such circumstances the local authority may give their *written consent* for the person to foster a child privately.

Regulations made under section 68 of the Act concerning disqualification are contained in Annex A to this volume.

Changes of Circumstances

1.6.8. Regulation 4 requires foster parents to notify the local authority in writing of certain changes in circumstance, in advance if practicable, but not more than 48 hours after the change; namely

- any change of the foster parent's address (if the foster parent moves to another local authority area — including Scotland — the authority receiving the notice shall inform the other local authority of the new address);
- the full name, sex, race, religion and date of birth of the child and the full name and address of

  (a) the parent(s)

  (b) any other person with parental responsibilities

  (c) any person from whom the child was, or is to be received;

- any person who begins or ceases to be part of his household;
- any new conviction, disqualification or prohibition of any person living in, or employed in the household;
- any subsequent proposals to foster a child privately,
- and in doing so shall specify the matters covered on Regulation 4(3)(a-f).

1.6.9. In notifying another local authority it is good practice to draw their attention to any important matters relating to the welfare of the child (eg a disability, difficulty or health problem) or the suitability of the foster parent. It is also good practice for the local authority to notify other agencies of the change, eg the health authority if the child has special health needs.

II Notification by Former Foster Parents

Timescale

1.6.10 . If the child moves, the former foster parents must notify their local authority in writing within 48 hours, stating the name and address of the person into whose care the child has been moved.

Reasons for Termination

1.6.11. The usual reason for terminating foster care is the return of the child to the parent.

1.6.12. If the child dies the foster parent must notify forthwith the local authority and the person from whom the child was received. Whether or not this person has parental responsibility, the local authority should ensure that the parent is notified forthwith. The local authority may need to assist the private foster parent with the formalities and in any event will need to consider the implications of what has happened.

1.6.13. If there are particular concerns about the death of a child there may be a need for the local authority to refer to the Area Child Protection Committee. (See Part 8 of 'Working Together' which provides further guidance on this subject).

Further Requirements

1.6.14. Under Regulation 6(4) any parent of a privately fostered child, and any other person who has parental responsibility for the child, shall notify the local authority in whose area the child was fostered of the ending of the fostering arrangement.

III Other Notifications

Person Involved in Fostering Arrangements

1.6.15. Under Regulation 6(1) the Act places a duty upon any other person (such as a third party) who is, or proposes to be, involved (whether or not directly) in arranging for a child to be fostered privately, to notify the local authority in whose area the child is to be fostered not less than 6 nor more than 13 weeks before commencement of arrangements.

Parental Duty

1.6.16. The Act places a new duty [Regulation 6(2)] on any parent, or person with parental responsibility for a child, to notify the local authority in whose area the child is proposed to be privately fostered, if he knows about the arrangement (even if he is not directly involved), not less than 6 and not more than 13 weeks before the fostering arrangement begins. The new requirement for a child's parent, and any other person, to notify the local authority is expected to ensure a greater degree of protection to children. Particular attention needs to be paid to this process.

Emergencies

1.6.17. The Regulations make provision for emergencies relating to notification of private fostering arrangements by parents and others involved in the placement, to be made not more than 48 hours following a placement.

Content of Notice

1.6.18. Specific details to be provided in the notification to local authorities by persons involved in private fostering arrangements is contained in Regulation 4(3).

Changes to Existing Arrangements

1.6.19. Under Regulation 6(4) any parent of a privately fostered child (and any other person who has parental responsibility for the child), must notify the local authority in whose area the child was privately fostered of any change in his address.

IV Form of Notifications

Requirements

1.6.20. In devising an efficient notification system local authorities should pay particular attention to:

- publicising and making available advice and information to prospective private foster parents, parents and others, on the requirement to notify;
- the design and content of notification forms to reflect the requirements of Regulations 4, 5 and 6;
- a common, reciprocal approach with other local authorities on the management of notifications when the proposed foster child is living in another local authority or, in another part of the United Kingdom.

V Notification Policy

Local Arrangements

1.6.21. While the duty to notify the local authority lies with the above persons specified in the Regulations, local authorities will need to have an effective policy for informing management and handling the notifications including their formal acknowledgement. Other agencies, particularly health visitors and schools, should be encouraged to liaise with social service departments about the existence of private foster children of whom the social services department may be unaware. This requires joint planning. In developing the policy, social services departments, together with other relevant agencies and departments in local authorities, should see their role as both regulatory and enabling with the aim of ensuring that the welfare of proposed, or actual, foster children is satisfactorily safeguarded and promoted.

1.6.22. In the event of non-notification, the local authority needs to establish agreed procedures with its legal department on how to handle offences under section 70 of the Act.

PART 1.7: WELFARE OF THE CHILD

Preparing the Ground

1.7.1. One of the key principles of the Children Act is that local authorities and health authorities should work in partnership to safeguard and promote the welfare of children in their area.

1.7.2. Private foster parents and the child's parents should be aware of the importance of continuity of health care, and, indeed, all aspects of the child's life, and share all relevant information. A child who is geographically mobile should not miss out on diagnosis and treatment that would satisfactorily safeguard and promote his welfare. Foster parents will need information about the child, the child's needs and history, medical background and the child's understanding of the reasons for and duration of the placement. Information on routines, capabilities, habits, fears, likes and dislikes and, where appropriate, sufficient information about the implications of a child's disability or learning difficulty, are essential if the foster parent is to offer good quality continuity of care and help the child settle into his new home. At the same time, the child should be told as much about the prospective foster parents as he is able to understand — eg interests of other children and location of the foster home.

1.7.3. The way the introduction to his new home is organised is important for the child's sense of security and acceptance of the change. A process of introduction helps to minimise the pain of separation. Foster parents need to be prepared for disturbed behaviour following such a change.

1.7.4. To secure the welfare of the child the foster parent will need in addition to the points raised in paragraph 1.7.2 above, a clear, preferably written, agreement with the child's parents on finances, pattern of contact with them and expected duration of placement.

Health

1.7.5. A child needs to be in good health in order to ensure that a private foster placement does not prejudice his welfare or educational experiences. Children of school age are included in health care provided under the School Health Service. Children aged under five who are privately fostered should not miss out on the child health surveillance programme. Health checks are usually offered at age 6 weeks, 8 months (range 7 to 9 months), 21 months (range 18 to 24 months), 39 months (range 36 to 42 months) and in some areas, entry at 5 years into school, (range 48 to 66 months). Private foster parents should make sure that they are informed by the child's parents about the child's health checks, vaccinations etc. (This schedule of surveillance checks is recommended in the report: 'Health for All Children' — Hall Report.)

1.7.6. Appropriate arrangements should also be made between the local authority, the foster parent and the child's parent for the PCHR to be held by the person who has care ('actual custody') of the child. All foster parents should have a working knowledge of, and skills in, first aid or be encouraged to obtain such knowledge and skills. Local branches of the Red Cross or St John Ambulance may offer useful sources of advice and training.

Child's Medical History

1.7.7. Inclusion of a child's medical history supports the notion of health care being an integral part of safeguarding and promoting the welfare of the child.

1.7.8. In addition to basic details of the child — height, weight, etc, details in a child's medical history should include:

(1) immunisations given and dates including, where practicable, the results of any neo-natal screening tests;

(2) history relating to infectious diseases, with dates;

(3) any episodes of in-patient or out-patient hospital treatment, for any condition with dates, giving details where possible;

(4) whether the child has, or is known to have, any congenital condition which has, or may have, medical implications and/or which necessitates ongoing health care;

(5) whether the child is known to have any allergies, including allergies to any medication;

(6) current short term or long term medication and other treatments, including consultants involved in the treatments;

(7) information on any special dietary requirements or dietary restrictions.

Consent to Medical Examination or Treatment

1.7.9. General medical consent, in respect of treatment for which the child himself is not capable of giving consent, to cover everyday treatment which may become necessary, should be given in writing to the private foster parent by the child's parent, or person with parental responsibility, at the commencement of the placement. It may be appropriate for the local authority and the health authority to have copies of the consent.

1.7.10. Children of sixteen and over give their own consent to medical treatment **(see also Health Circular HC(90)22, Health Service Management: Patient Consent to Treatment or Examination)**. Children under sixteen may also be able to give or refuse consent depending on their capacity to understand the nature of the treatment; it is for the doctor to decide this. Children who are judged able to give consent cannot be medically examined or treated without their consent. The child's attention should be drawn to his rights to give or refuse consent to examination or treatment if he is 16 or over or if he is under 16 and the doctor considers him to be capable of sufficient understanding to give or withold consent to the treatment in question. Young people should be encouraged to understand the importance of health care and to take responsibility for their own health. The recent decision of the Court of Appeal (in Re R 31 July 1991, Times Law Reports) would suggest that if a child refuses consent and parents or others with parental responsibility wish to contest this, they should seek legal advice about applying to the court to exercise its inherent jurisdiction requiring that the child should be made party to such proceedings.

Registration with General Medical Practitioner

1.7.11. Regulation 2(2)(f) requires that a privately fostered child should be included on the list of a general medical practitioner. Ideally, the child should remain with the present GP, if possible. Local authorities should ensure, in partnership with the FHSA, that all privately fostered children are so registered. The child's parent, or person with parental responsibility for the child, should be given the name and address of the general medical practitioner with whom the child is registered. Regular visits to the dentist for checks and treatment should form an integral part of the general health care of the child.

Medical Examinations

1.7.12. It is recommended good practice that, as with all children who live away from home, medical examinations should be arranged for a privately fostered child when he commences placement, or as soon as it is practicable to do so thereafter. Where a child has an incomplete medical history a requirement may be made under paragraph (6)(1)(c) of Schedule 8 for further medical examinations to be carried out at specified periods. The medical officer may charge the natural parent for these examinations.

Services for Children with Disabilities

1.7.13. Section 17(11) of the Act defines disablement in a child as follows:

"A child is disabled if he is blind or dumb or suffers from mental disorder of any kind or is substantially and permanently handicapped by illness, injury or congenital deformity or such other disability as may be prescribed," [section 17(11)].

1.7.14. Schedule 2, paragraph 2(2) requires local authorities to open and maintain a register of disabled children in their area. Schedule 2, paragraph 6 of the Act places a separate duty on local authorities to provide services for children with disabilities designed to minimise the effect of their disabilities and give such children the opportunity to lead lives as normal as possible. The register and services should help in the identification, diagnosis, assessment and treatment of privately fostered children with a physical and mental handicap or mental disorder and in overcoming limitations of mobility and communication. This may include provision of equipment such as communication aids and interpreters.

1.7.15. In co-operation with relevant agencies, authorities will need to consider the overall development needs of a child who is privately fostered. Advice and help on home aids, equipment and adaptations can be obtained from the Disabled Living Foundation of the Royal Association for Disability and Rehabilitation. More detailed guidance is contained in Volume 6: 'Children with Disabilities'.

Female Circumcision

1.7.16. Regulation 2(2)(c) requires local authorities to satisfy themselves that a privately fostered child's needs arising from his religious persuasion, racial origin and cultural background are being met. In certain circumstances where children of particular ethnic minority and cultural backgrounds are privately fostered, local authorities, in co-operation with health authorities, will need to concern themselves with certain religious or cultural practices which are prohibited within the United Kingdom.

1.7.17. For example, female circumcision, excision and infibulation ('female genital mutilation') is an offence under the Prohibition of Female Circumcision Act 1985. The Act makes certain exceptions from criminal liability, for example where the operation is considered necessary for the child's physical or mental health. However, the 1985 Act specifies that on no account should physical or mental health be a consideration for the operation in matters of custom or ritual. Parents should not be encouraged in their belief that they can escape the penalties of the criminal law by allowing circumcision because they consider it would benefit their child's health.

1.7.18. In circumstances where a local authority has reason to believe that a child is likely to suffer significant harm as a result of female circumcision they should exercise their powers to investigate under section 47 of the 1989 Act and consider the need to exercise any of their powers, for example under Part V (emergency protection).

1.7.19. In areas where there are significant numbers of privately fostered children of particular ethnic minority or cultural background, local authorities and health authorities, directly managed units/NHS trusts will need to alert social workers, GPs and health visitors to the possibility of female circumcision. Advice on this matter can be obtained from the Foundation for Womens Health Research and Development (FORWARD) at the Africa Centre in London or from School of Oriental and African Studies, University of London.

Male Circumcision

1.7.20. Other than meeting the needs of therapeutic requirements, male circumcision is a religious, social and cultural practice among many groups in the United Kingdom, and is not restricted to a particular ethnic or cultural minority. The operation is simple and straight forward and should, under appropriate conditions, pose no harm or danger to the health and welfare of the child. If, however, a parent requests a private foster parent to arrange circumcision, the foster parent should be advised that circumcision should be carried out in an environment which provides adequate safeguards by a properly qualified medical practitioner at a hospital or clinic.

Race, Culture, Religion and Linguistic Needs

1.7.21. In seeking to satisfy themselves that a child's welfare is being satisfactorily safeguarded and promoted in the private foster home, social workers need to be aware and establish that the private foster parent is aware of differences between minority group children and the significance of religion and culture in relation to racial origin. It should not be assumed that the parent of the child and the private foster parent will have the same religion or share the same cultural background.

1.7.22. The quality and consistency of care a child receives in his formative years is crucial to his physical, intellectual, emotional, social and behavioural development. The practice among some ethnic minority families to place their children in private foster homes of a different race and culture may, in some instances, pose a contradiction for local authorities when carrying out their functions under Regulation 2(2)(c). In such circumstances the local authority should seek to establish the prospective foster parent's understanding of the child's culture and the level of his willingness to do so.

1.7.23. Local authorities are encouraged to see that the foster parent is advised about the provision of resources and facilities which could assist him meet the racial, cultural, religious and linguistic needs of the child. This can be done, for example, by involving the voluntary sector, local religious groups and minority ethnic communities. The services of an interpreter may sometimes be required if foster parents do not have sufficient communication skills in the child's language.

1.7.24. Local authorities will need to be aware of the practical difficulties which such placements can present and be prepared to deal with them at an early stage to avoid problems for the future. However, the fact that such placements are by private arrangement means that local authorities should not be seeking to prevent them because of potential difficulties, save where other considerations justify the imposition of requirements or a prohibition, and be prepared to deal with them at an early stage to avoid problems for the future.

Needs of Siblings

1.7.25. The social worker should ensure that adequate arrangements are made for relationships between siblings to develop. Arrangements for the care of any brothers and sisters not included in the proposed or actual foster arrangement need to be notified to the local authority [Regulation 6(3)(b)].

Equal Opportunities

1.7.26. Section 71 of the Race Relations Act gives local authorities a duty to promote good race relations. Local authorities should have approved equal opportunities policies. Private foster parents who are caring for children from a particular ethnic minority, or cultural group, should be encouraged to value and respect a child's racial origins, religion, culture and language. Local authorities will have to consider how advice and knowledge on equal opportunities, cultural issues, childcare and health matters can be shared with private foster parents. Further information and guidance on race equality, policies and ethnic monitoring is available from the Commission for Racial Equality.

1.7.27. Local authorities, in consultation with their legal departments, should ensure that appropriate procedures are made for dealing with children who are privately fostered. All procedures should aim to ensure that agency services do not reflect or reinforce social and economic disadvantage, or discrimination, in a child's life.

Continuity and Change

1.7.28. Advice to private foster parents and natural parents should include the importance of planned endings to fostering arrangements and preparing the child for the change. This is particularly important where the child is to move to new foster parents and the local authority may decide to support a short term placement under section 17 of the Act if a child is in need, to give space for preparation and introductory visits.

1.7.29. As much continuity as possible should be maintained, eg continuing at the same school, remaining with the same G.P., providing information on background, habits, interests, routines and needs. Also, private foster parents should be encouraged to maintain a photograph album for the child and a diary of significant events which the child can keep when he moves on.

1.7.30. A child's return to his family may also need careful preparation by both the foster parent and the child's parent, depending on the length of time the child has been away and the extent of changes within the family. Some children are intentionally placed in private foster care on a long term basis in the belief that it is good to grow up in a white family. This can create a serious dilemna for the child when it is time for him to return home.

1.7.31. The need for continuity is equally critical at the end of the placement as at the beginning. Children often return to different addresses, an unfamiliar culture and new family members. The former foster parents should be advised to pass on information to the parent on the habits, food preferences, interests, routines and connections developed by the child. Ideally, parents should be prepared for these changes and the possibility of disturbed behaviour while the child re-establishes himself in his family.

1.7.32. The private foster parent should always obtain the agreement of the natural parent prior to any move to another private foster parent. Depending on the circumstances the authority may need to consider contacting, consulting or advising the natural parent directly, particularly as many "emergency" moves arise from disharmony between the natural parent and foster parent, or disturbed behaviour on the part of the child.

Recording the Child's Development

1.7.33. It is good practice for the local authority social worker to offer private foster parents advice about the information they should keep and the manner in which they should keep it, to be shared with the parents, and where appropriate, the local authority social services, health and education services. Such advice should cover.

— maintaining and updating the child's medical history, (with appropriate input from health personnel) and include notes/dates of visits to the GP, health clinic etc;

— keeping a file of school reports;

— noting the dates and means of contact with the parents and other significant people in the child's life (visits, letters, phone calls);

— maintaining a financial record of monies received on behalf of the child's upkeep;

— noting the dates and nature of social services contact;

— keeping a photograph album of significant events/people in the child's life.

PART 1.8: THE ROLE OF LOCAL AUTHORITIES

Local Authority Powers

1.8.1. Paragraph 6 of Schedule 8 gives power to local authorities to impose requirements. These can be related to an individual or category of children, eg those over a certain age.

1.8.2. In any event reasons must be given for the imposition of requirements. The recipient has 14 days from when the notice is served to appeal to the court. It is therefore advisable to inform the private foster parent that a requirement is to be made in order to give time for any informal negotiations or accommodations to take place if it is consistant with the welfare of the child, thus preventing unnecessary appeals to court.

1.8.3. A requirement does not have effect while an appeal is pending. A court may dismiss the appeal or if not, can cancel, vary or allow more tine for compliance.

1.8.4. Decisions to impose requirements should be taken by the authority in accordance with established procedures. The local authority has the power to remove, vary, or add requirements and will need to have a policy on how these decisions are to be made.

Supervisory Visits

1.8.5. Regulation 3 lays down the minimum visiting requirements by a local authority to the private foster home. The frequency of visits should be determined by the circumstances of the case but should not be below the requirements specified in Regulation 3. The authority must arrange a visit whenever reasonably requested by a child or foster parent. The minimum visiting requirements imposed on local authorities are set out in Regulation 3(1) (a) and (b).

1.8.6. Visits should not be neglected because a placement is going well or is difficult. The social worker will not be equipped to identify, help or assess fully long term situations if no care has been taken to establish a relationship with a child and foster parent.

1.8.7. Care needs to be taken to maintain the delicate balance between meeting the purpose of the visit and satisfying the regulations without unsettling the placement to the detriment of the child. This is easier where a way of working in partnership has been established at the beginning. The social worker should make clear to the foster parent the purpose of the visit and the areas about which the local authority needs to be satisfied.

Purpose of Visits

1.8.8. The purpose of visits include

(i) child protection. The overall standard of care should be observed. The child's bedroom should be seen on some visits, especially if there has been any change in the arrangements. If the local authority considers it appropriate, some visits should be unannounced. Occasionally other visits should take place when all members of the household are likely to be at home. The child, parent and foster parent should feel free to get in touch with the social worker at any time;

(ii) providing a link. The social worker's visits can provide encouragement to the maintenance or improvement of child care standards, taking account of Regulation 2;

(iii) a check that any requirements are being met and whether they need to be changed or cancelled;

(iv) ensuring that the foster parent receives necessary advice from the social worker or others, eg health visitor, G.P., Education, Welfare Rights etc. This advice can be given individually or in groups;

(v) enquiring how the arrangements with the natural parent are working and consider whether it would be appropriate for the local authority to intervene;

(vii) satisfying the local authority that the welfare of the child is satisfactory.

Seeing the Child Alone

1.8.9. The first time the child is seen is often on the first supervisory visit. A check should be made to see if he is in need as defined under Part III of the Act and the provision of any services facilitated. The child must be seen at each visit. The Regulations provide for the child to be seen alone if considered necessary by the local authority. If desired, it should be carried out outside the foster home.

1.8.10. It is also important to check with the child, as far as practicable, that the fostering arrangements are in place and schooling and health care are being satisfactorily provided, and to advise on any settling-in difficulties. Guidance following an unsatisfactory care report is contained in paragraphs 1.8.13–1.8.17 below.

Written Reports

1.8.11. After each visit, the local authority is required to ensure that the social worker who made the visit produces a written report. The report should indicate whether the child was seen and, if not, the reasons and also whether the child was seen alone. It should also comment on the child's welfare and if the placement is satisfactory, including any comments made by the child or the carer. Any matter for concern or difficulty should be highlighted so that the need for any action can be discussed with the social worker's supervisor.

1.8.12. The framework of the report should be designed with a view to the local authority taking one, or a combination of, the following courses of action:

● impose one or more requirements under Schedule 8, paragraph 6 on the person who is or proposes to foster the child privately;

● impose a prohibition under section 69 on the person who is or proposes to foster the child privately;

● impose a prohibition *with* conditions upon non-compliance with requirements under section 69(5) on the person who is or proposes to foster the child privately;

● consider to what extent they should exercise any of their functions pursuant to section 67(5) of the Act with respect to the child.

Unsatisfactory Care

1.8.13. Decisions under section 67(5) of the Act should not be taken by the social worker working alone. If there is "reasonable cause to suspect that the child is suffering, or is likely to suffer, significant harm" the child protection procedures under Part V of the Act should be invoked immediately. This is the only way the local authority can seek to move the child against the private foster parent's wishes. (The natural parent can do so and can be so advised, but the foster parent can seek to prevent this by applying for a residence order or adoption after 5 years without parental consent). Otherwise, concerns should be discussed with senior managers or a panel of officers that monitor standards, together with the authority's legal advisers. Authorities need to be clear about the level at which care becomes unsatisfactory. In any event, the local authority should take action to inform the parent of any unsatisfactory case revealed to them.

1.8.14. Having clarified the areas of concern, various options need to be considered, bearing in mind that delay is usually contrary to the best interest of the child. If the child is "in need" as defined by Part 3, section 17 of the Act, the authority may consider whether temporary help, including financial help, should be made available in the short term to give time for the child to be prepared for any move or for the placement to be brought up to standard, should a move be contrary to the best interest of the child. This also gives time for the natural parent to be informed of the situation by the local authority and be able to come to a considered decision.

1.8.15. If the decision is that the child's welfare cannot be satisfactorily safeguarded or promoted in the foster home then, as long as it is in the child's best interest, the local authority should seek to have his care and accommodation undertaken by a parent or a person with parental responsibility. The Act also gives the local authority power to secure that care and accommodation is undertaken by a relative. This should be with the agreement of the parent, or if the parent cannot be found, after the suitability of the relative has been assessed. The local authority can either an over responsibility for the child to the relative or consider accommodating the child under section 20 of the Act or offering support under section 17 of the Act.

1.8.16. A child will need help to cope with a.disrupted placement and will need reassurance that he is not to blame, if this is the case. The natural parent should be involved in, or at least be informed of any significant action taken by the local authority. The natural parent can at any time during the placement remove the child from the foster home.

1.8.17. There may be particular difficulties if the child's parent is overseas. The short term expenses of rehabilitating the child with his natural family may be more cost effective than long term local authority care if it is judged to be in the child's best interests but the local authority will need to be clear about these issues and the need to obtain court authority if the child is to live overseas (see Part 9: International Aspects.)

Refusal to Allow Visits

1.8.18. It is an offence for a foster parent to refuse to allow a child to be visited or to obstruct an authorised officer, who has reasonable cause to believe that a privately fostered child is being accommodated within the authority's area, from any exercise of any duty towards the child. An officer encountering any difficulties should discuss the problem with senior staff and legal advisors.

After Care

1.8.19. Local authorities are given new responsibilities towards certain privately fostered children who have left their foster home. A disabled person who is under 21 and who was (but is no longer) privately fostered at any time after his sixteenth birthday qualifies for advice and assistance from the local authority in whose area he is [section 24(2)(e)].

1.8.20. The local authority may advise, assist and befriend such a person if he asks for help and his foster parents do not have the necessary facilities to advise or befriend him [section 24(4)–(6)]. Assistance may be in kind or, in exceptional circumstances, in cash [section 24(7)] which may also be conditional on repayment, except where a person is in receipt of income support or family credit, [section 24(10)]. If the person who has been advised or befriended lives in another authority's area, or proposes to live there, the local authority must inform that other local authority [section 24(11)3].

1.8.21. The guidance in Volume 3, Chapter 9, 'After-Care: Advice and Assistance' includes reference to private foster children and should be consulted for guidance on principles and practice. It is important to note that only general subsections of section 24 of the Act apply to private fostering.

Those that refer only to children formerly looked after or accommodated by specific authorities or organisations do not.

Prohibitions

1.8.22. Section 69(1), (2) and (3) provides local authorities with the power to prohibit a person from privately fostering children where they are of the opinion that:

(a) he is not a suitable person [section 69(2) (a)];

(b) the premises are not suitable [section 69(2)(b)];

(c) neither the person nor the accommodation is suitable [section 69(2)(c)].

1.8.23. Local authorities will, in consultation with their legal departments, wish to develop a general policy on the use of this power so that prohibitions provide an effective framework for promoting and safeguarding the welfare of children, and to prevent unsuitable persons privately fostering children in accommodation that would be prejudicial to the child's welfare.

1.8.24. The power of the local authority to impose a prohibition on a person applies to person's who propose to foster privately, as well as to a person who is actually fostering a child privately [section 69(1]. Under this power the local authority may impose a general prohibition on a person, which applies to any child in any accommodation within the area of the local authority [section 69(3)(a)]. In addition, the local authority may make the prohibition specific to any child in particular accommodation [section 69(3)(b)], or to a named child in particular accommodation [section 69(3)(c)].

1.8.25. Section 69(5) gives local authorities power to impose requirements under Schedule 8 paragraph 6., which is to be distinguished from a prohibition on a person who proposes to foster privately, or is fostering a child privately. This power should assist the local authority to fulfil its duty to safeguard and promote the welfare of privately fostered children in its area.

1.8.26. A prohibition must be in writing, sent to the person on whom it is being imposed and specify reasons, contain information about the right of the person to appeal and the time in which he may do so [section 69(7)].

1.8.27. In circumstances where a prohibition is imposed on a private foster parent, the local authority should exercise its duty under section 67(1) and satisfy themselves that the child's welfare is protected by the foster parents.

Cancellation of Prohibitions

1.8.28. Section 69(4) give local authorities the power to cancel a prohibition. This power is provided so that local authorities can respond appropriately to matters raised during the process of conducting enquiries into the suitability of the person and his accommodation; or to changes notified by the person.

1.8.29. Persons on whom a prohibition has been imposed under Section 69 are disqualified from private fostering and from carrying on or being employed in a children's home, voluntary home, day care or childminding, (Disqualification for Caring for Children Regulations 1991).

Offences

1.8.30. Section 70 covers offences in relation to private fostering.

● In the case of the offence of looking after children whilst disqualified from private fostering, or whilst prohibited, a person found guilty on summary conviction would be liable to a term of imprisonment of not more than six months or a fine or both. For all other offences the penalty would be a fine.

● It is an offence for a person under paragraph 10 of Schedule 8 to publish an advertisement offering to undertake or arrange for a child to be privately fostered unless it states that person's name and address.

25

- In cases where a person is privately fostering, or proposes to foster privately more than three children at any one time, the person will be required to register as "a children's home" [section 63]. Any person caring for and accommodating children in a children's home which is not registered, if found guilty on summary conviction, is liable to a fine. Exceptionally, local authorities may exempt a person from registering as "a children's home" under paragraph 4 of Schedule 7. (Further guidance on foster placements is contained in Volume 3, 'Family Placements', page 34).

1.8.31. Transitional provisions under paragraph 32 of Schedule 14 to the Act concerning foster parents with more than three foster children, allow 3 months within which an application can be made to register the home as a children's home. During that time the local authority can consider the alternative, an exercise of discretion under Schedule 7, to exempt the foster parents from the usual fostering limit.

1.8.32. Where day care for children under eight is provided by a person for more than two hours a day, and for more than 6 days in any year, and for reward, that person shall need to register as a child minder.

1.8.33. It is important for local authorities to ensure that a person who plans to undertake child minding and/or privately foster children under eight clearly understands that under Part X of the Act he is required to *register*, and under Part IX of the Act he is required to *notify* the local authority of his proposal to foster a child privately.

Appeals

1.8.34. Schedule 8, paragraph 8 covers appeals by a person who is, or proposes to, foster a child privately under Part X or wishes to challenge the local authority's decision not to exempt them from exceeding the fostering limit of 3 children under paragraph 4 of Schedule 7.

- Schedule 6 paragraph 8 covers appeals by a person who is carrying on "a children's home".

Local Authority Approach to Private Fostering

1.8.35. The Children Act uses the term 'parental responsibility' to describe the duties, rights and authority which a parent has in respect of his child, including a child who is privately fostered. The component parts of the term emphasise the fundamental tasks of parenthood.

1.8.36. Ensuring basic standards for children who are privately fostered is a public responsibility . Part IX of the Act [section 67(1)] requires local authorities to ensure that advice is given to those persons caring for and accommodating children who are privately fostered. This is particularly important for the care and protection of children.

1.8.37. Local authorities will need to review their existing child care policy towards children who are proposed to be, or are being, privately fostered. Their priorities will need to be re-examined and in the light of the current regulations and guidance. There will be a need to re-evaluate the operation of their duties and powers towards privately fostered children, particularly so in relation to initiating notification, decision making, information and visiting. In the course of putting these into operation, local authorities will also have to take note of paragraph 1(1) of Schedule 2 to the Act and the requirements to take reasonable steps to identify the extent of children *in need* in their area.

1.8.38. Local authorities and other relevant agencies will be responsible for decisions about their own arrangements for managing the legal and administrative issues assigned to them under the Act. They should establish that those proposing to care for privately fostered children know where they can get information about obtaining appropriate advice and assistance from other agencies. Similarly, they should be encouraged to work with other key agencies in meeting the legitimate needs of privately fostered children, their parents and private foster parents.

1.8.39. Local authorities will, therefore, need to reappraise their organisational arrangements and interactive links between their own and other social services departments, legal departments, education and health departments and other agencies in order to carry out their duties in satisfying themselves that the welfare of privately fostered children is safeguarded and promoted. These links in many cases will be the same as those in existence, or being set up in respect of collaborative working, to meet the requirements of the new legislation.

PART 1.9: INTERNATIONAL ASPECTS

Immigration and Nationality

1.9.1. There is no provision in the Immigration Rules for children to be admitted to the United Kingdom for private fostering. However, foreign nationals and Commonwealth citizens who are admitted to the United Kingdom for a limited period, for example as visitors, students or work permit holders, may be joined or accompanied by their children provided that certain conditions are met (for example, the parents must be able to maintain and accommodate their children adequately without recourse to public funds). There is no objection to parents placing their children in private foster care during their stay in the United Kingdom provided that they take the child with them when they leave the country. Children will normally be given leave to remain for the same period as their parents. The date when the child's leave to remain expires will be stamped in the child's passport on arrival in the United Kingdom.

1.9.2. Any person who has limited leave to remain in the United Kingdom must leave the country before his or her leave expires. If he does not do so, he will automatically become an overstayer, which is a criminal offence, and is liable to be removed from the United Kingdom. An application may be made to the Home Office Immigration and Nationality Department for an extension of leave to remain, and a child whose parents were still lawfully present in the United Kingdom would normally be allowed further leave to remain for the same period as the parents. It should be noted that any application for an extension of leave to remain *must* be made before the child's current leave expires; and that there is no provision in the Immigration Rules for a person who was admitted for 6 months as a visitor to be granted further leave to remain as a visitor or a student.

1.9.3. A child born in the United Kingdom prior to 1 January 1983 is a British citizen and is not therefore subject to immigration control. A child born in the United Kingdom after that date will be a British citizen if at the time of his or her birth his father or mother is a British citizen or lawfully settled in the United Kingdom. A new born child who is found abandoned in the United Kingdom is assumed to meet the above requirements unless the contrary is shown.

1.9.4. A local authority or private foster parent who are in any doubt about a child's immigration or nationality status are strongly advised to consult the Home Office Immigration and Nationality Department at the earliest opportunity. Where a foreign child is abandoned in a private foster home in the United Kingdom, local authorities can also seek assistance from the International Social Services with a view to tracing the child's parents and arranging for the child to be returned to them.

Living Abroad

1.9.5. A parent of a child who is being privately fostered, or person with parental responsibility for him, can arrange for his return to his own country from the United Kingdom, sometimes in opposition of the wishes of the child himself or in opposition to the wishes of the private foster parent. It would be advisable for local authorities to establish, in so far as it is practicable to do so, whether the child's parent and the private foster parent know of any plans for the child to emigrate. This will avoid frustrations that may arise from mistaken, confused or disappointed expectations about any proposed or actual plans for the child to emigrate.

1.9.6. Where arrangements need to be made for children whose families live abroad, this is primarily a matter for the foster parent and the parent. However, if the placement has broken down and the child is accommodated by the local authority, the authority may need to assist with travel arrangements.

1.9.7. Under Schedule 2 paragraph 19(2) local authorities may arrange (or assist in making arrangements) for a child for whom they are providing accommodation by voluntary agreement to live outside England and Wales with the approval of each person who has parental responsibility for the child. Where a child, including a child who had previously been fostered privately, is looked after by a local authority, the court's approval must be sought [Schedule 2 paragraph 19(1)]. This may only be given in certain circumstances where:

- the child himself consents (if he has sufficient understanding) (Schedule 2(19) (3);
- suitable arrangements have been made for the reception and welfare of the child in the new country which would be in the child's best interests, (Schedule 2 paragraph 19(4);
- each person with parental responsibility for the child consents or his consent is dispensed with (Schedule 2 paragraph 19(5).

Admission to Schools of Children from Overseas

1.9.8. The following information has been provided by the Department of Education and Science and forms part of their guidance concerning the admission to county and voluntary schools of children from overseas, (Circular No 11/88: 20 October 1988).

1.9.9. There are no restrictions on entry to the United Kingdom to children who hold full British citizen passports or children from Commonwealth countries whose passport have been endorsed to show that they have the right of abode in the United Kingdom. Such children, having entered, are entitled to study at a county or voluntary school, subject to normal school admission requirements.

1.9.10. Holders of passports describing them as British Dependent Territories Citizens or British Overseas Citizens have no automatic entitlement to the right of abode in the United Kingdom and therefore no right of entry in order to attend county or voluntary schools.

Visitors to the United Kingdom

1.9.11. The circumstances in which children are admitted to this country with their parents as visitors (and as such are here for a limited stay) will obviously vary, as the parents may be here for a few days holiday or several months stay. Each application for admission will need to be considered on its merits in the light of the practicability of providing a place and the expediency of doing so (in terms of the educational welfare of the child). The likely length of stay of the child in this country will clearly need to be taken into account; under the Immigration Rules the maximum length of stay allowed to a visitor is six months.

1.9.12. The decision whether or not to admit a child to a county or voluntary school is a matter for authorities (and governors where they are responsible for admissions) in the light of their statutory duties and subject to any decision by an appeal committee constituted under section 7 of the Education Act

1980. However, should a complaint be made by parents to the Secretary of State for Education and Science that a child has been refused admission to such a school merely on the grounds that he was likely to be in the area for a short time (however that period may be defined), the Secretary of State would be bound to investigate the case on its merits and, if he was satisfied that the authority's or governor's action amounted to a failure to discharge a duty laid upon them, could direct that the child be so admitted.

PART 1.10: RECORDS TO BE KEPT BY LOCAL AUTHORITIES

Contents

1.10.1. Accurate, comprehensive and well organised records are essential to good practice. Careful recording of agreements and decisions relating to the placement of the child, including the aim of the placement and the child's progress should be monitored and kept under regular review. They are the basis, as social workers and careers change, for a clear and common understanding of the plan for the child, the arrangements made, agreements reached, decisions made and the reasons for them.

Case Records

1.10.2. The records should be such as to trace without difficulty the process of decision-making so that the views of the child and his parents can be easily found and related to the sequence of decisions taken and arrangements made.

Safekeeping

1.10.3. Good practice requires authorities to take steps to ensure the safekeeping of records. This requires not only arrangements for the physical security of the records but effective procedures to restrict access to the records only to those who are properly authorised and in need of information because of their duties in relation to a case.

Access to Records

1.10.4. Local authorities should act in accordance with the guidance contained in Volume 3, 'Guidance and Regulations concerning Family Placements, paragraphs 1.2.85 and 1.2.86. They should also seek the advice of their own legal advisers concerning the disclosure of information held. It is good practice that information held about an individual should be shared with him unless there are special reasons for withholding it covered by the legislation and guidance mentioned.

Retention of Records

1.10.5. The length of time recommended for the retention of records by local authorities relating to private foster placements has not been specified. However, it would be good practice if the timescales which were applied to these records were the same, where appropriate, as those specified for placements arranged by local authorities in Statutory Instrument SI 1991 No 890, paragraph (1): 'A case record relating to a child who is placed shall be retained by the responsible authority until the seventy-fifth anniversary of the date of birth of the child to whom it relates or, if the child dies before attaining the age of 18, for a period of 15 years beginning with the date of his death'.

(c) the purpose and intended duration of the fostering arrangement;

(d) the name and address of any parent of the child and of any other person who has parental responsibility for the child and (if different) of any person from whom the child was, or is to be, received;

(e) the name and address of any person, other than a person specified in sub-paragraph (d) above, who is involved directly or indirectly in making the fostering arrangement; and

(f) the intended date of the beginning of the fostering arrangement or, as the case may be, the date on which the arrangement actually began.

(4) A person giving notice under paragraph (1) or (2) shall include in the notice particulars of–

(a) any offence of which he has been convicted;

(b) any disqualification or prohibition imposed on him under (as the case may be) section 68 or 69 of the Act or under any previous enactment of either of those sections; and

(c) any such conviction, disqualification or prohibition imposed on any other person living in, or employed at, the same household.

(5) Any person who is fostering a child privately shall notify the appropriate local authority of–

(a) any change in his address;

(b) any person who begins, or ceases, to be part of his household; and

(c) any further conviction, disqualification or prohibition as mentioned in sub-paragraphs (a) to (c) of paragraph (4).

(6) A notice under paragraph (5) shall be given–

(a) in advance if practicable; and

(b) in any other case, not more than 48 hours after the change of circumstances,

and if the new address is in the area of another local authority, or of a local authority in Scotland, the authority to whom the notice is given shall inform the other authority of the new address and of the particulars given to them under sub-paragraphs (a) and (d) of paragraph (3).

(7) Paragraphs (4)(a) and (c) and (5)(c) are subject to the Rehabilitation of Offenders Act 1974(a).

Notifications by former foster parents

5.—(1) Subject to paragraphs (2) and (3), any person who has been fostering a child privately, but has ceased to do so, shall notify the appropriate local authority within 48 hours and shall include in the notice the name and address of the person into whose care the child was received.

(2) Where the reason for the ending of the fostering arrangement is the death of the child the foster parent shall notify forthwith the local authority and also the person from whom the foster parent received the child.

(3) Paragraph (1) shall not apply where the foster parent intends to resume the fostering arrangement after an interval of not more than 27 days but if–

(a) he subsequently abandons his intention; or

(b) the interval expires without his having given effect to his intention,

he shall thereupon give notice to the local authority within 48 hours of abandoning his intention or as the case may be the expiry of the interval.

Other notifications

6.—(1) Any person who is, or proposes to be, involved (whether or not directly) in arranging for a child to be fostered privately shall notify the appropriate local authority not less than six, nor more than thirteen, weeks before the fostering arrangement begins

---

(a) 1974 c.53.

unless the fostering arrangement is made in an emergency in which case the notification shall be not more than 48 hours after the fostering arrangement begins.

(2) A parent of a child, and any other person who has parental responsibility for the child, who knows that it is proposed that the child should be fostered privately shall notify the appropriate local authority not less than six, nor more than thirteen, weeks before the fostering arrangement begins unless the fostering arrangement is made in an emergency in which case the notification shall be not more than 48 hours thereafter.

(3) Any notice under paragraph (1) or (2) shall specify–

    (a) the information mentioned in sub-paragraphs (a) to (c) of regulation 4(3);

    (b) the arrangements for the care of any brother or sister of the child who is not included in the fostering arrangement;

    (c) the name and address of any other person involved (whether or not directly) in the fostering arrangement;

    (d) where the notice is given under paragraph (1), the relationship to the child of the person giving the notice and also the information specified in sub-paragraph (d) of regulation 4(3).

(4) Any parent of a privately fostered child, and any other person who has parental responsibility for the child, shall notify the appropriate local authority of–

    (a) the ending of the fostering arrangement; and

    (b) any change in his own address.

Form of notifications

7. Any notice required under regulations 4 to 6 shall be given in writing and may be sent by post.

Signed by authority of the Secretary of State for Health.

Virginia Bottomley
Minister of State,
Department of Health

10th September 1991

EXPLANATORY NOTE

(This note is not part of the Regulations)

These Regulations provide for the arrangements for fostering children privately. Such arrangements were previously governed by provisions of the Foster Children Act 1980 (c.6). The main difference between the provisions under the 1980 Act and the Children Act 1989, under which these Regulations are made, is that much of the detail concerning notification, visiting and the local authority's welfare duty towards privately fostered children which was contained in the 1980 Act is now contained with modifications in these Regulations rather than the 1989 Act.

The Regulations make provision for the matters as to which local authorities are required to satisfy themselves regarding the welfare of privately fostered children (regulation 2); for the occasions on which officers of the authorities are to visit privately fostered children (regulation 3); as to notifications by prospective and actual foster parents (regulation 4) and by former foster parents (regulation 5); and as to other notifications (regulation 6) and to the form of notifications (regulation 7) (failure to comply with the provisions for notification may be an offence under section 70(1)(a) of the Children Act 1989).

£1.00 net

ISBN 0 11 015050 3

Printed in the United Kingdom for HMSO
879   WO1777   C40   9/91   452/3   4235   134976   913741

STATUTORY INSTRUMENTS

1991 No. 2094

CHILDREN AND YOUNG PERSONS

The Disqualification for Caring for Children Regulations 1991

Made - - - -	*17th September 1991*
Laid before Parliament	*23rd September 1991*
Coming into force -	*14th October 1991*

The Secretary of State for Health in relation to England and Wales in exercise of the powers conferred by section 68(1) and (2) of and paragraph 8 of Schedule 5 and paragraph 2 of Schedule 9 to the Children Act 1989(a) and the Secretary of State for Scotland in relation to Scotland in exercise of the powers conferred by the said paragraph 2 of Schedule 9 and, in each case, of all other powers enabling them in that behalf hereby make the following Regulations:–

Citation commencement interpretation and extent

  1.—(1) These Regulations may be cited as the Disqualification for Caring for Children Regulations 1991 and shall come into force on 14th October 1991.

  (2) In these Regulations unless the context otherwise requires–
   (a) "the Act" means the Children Act 1989;
   (b) any reference to a Schedule is to the Schedule to these Regulations.

  (3) These Regulations extend to Scotland only in so far as they provide for disqualification from registration under Part X of the Act (childminding and day care).

Disqualification from fostering a child privately or registration under Part X of the Act

  2. For the purpose of section 68 (persons disqualified from being private foster parents) and of paragraph 2 of Schedule 9 to the Act (disqualification from registration), a person is disqualified from fostering a child privately or registering under section 71 of the Act (registration for child-minding and day-care) if–
   (a) he is a parent of a child who at any time has been made the subject of an order under section 31(1)(a) of the Act (care order);
   (b) one of the following orders has been made at any time with respect to a child so as to remove the child from his care or prevent the child living with him–
    (i) an order under section 31(1)(a) of the Act or an order under section 1(3)(c) or 7(7)(a) of the Children and Young Persons Act 1969(b) (care orders),
    (ii) any other order that would have been deemed to be a care order by virtue of paragraph 15 of Schedule 14 to the Act (transitional provisions for

---

(a) 1989 c.41. Paragraph 2 of Schedule 9 to the Children Act 1989 was amended by paragraph 30 of Schedule 16 to the Courts and Legal Services Act 1990 (c.41).
(b) 1969 c.54.

children in compulsory care) had it been in force immediately before the day on which Part IV of the Act comes into force,

    (iii) a supervision order which imposes a residence requirement under section 12AA of the Children and Young Persons Act 1969**(a)** (requirement that young offender live in local authority accommodation),

    (iv) an approved school order or a fit person order under section 9(1)(a) or (b) of the Children and Young Persons Act 1933**(b)** or section 61(1)(a) or (b) of the Children and Young Persons (Scotland) Act 1937**(c)**, or

    (v) a fit person order, parental rights order or a training school order under the Children and Young Persons Act (Northern Ireland) 1968**(d)**, or the Children and Young Persons Act (Northern Ireland) 1950**(e)**;

(c) a supervision requirement has been imposed under the Social Work (Scotland) Act 1968**(f)** at any time with respect to any child for the purpose of removing that child from his care;

(d) his rights and powers with respect to the child had at any time been vested in a local authority in Scotland under the Social Work (Scotland) Act 1968 or the Children Act 1948**(g)**;

(e) an order has been made at any time, for the purposes of removing a child who was being kept, or was about to be received, by him, under–

    (i) section 34 of the Adoption Act 1976**(h)** or section 43 of the Adoption Act 1958**(i)** (removal of protected children from unsuitable surroundings),

    (ii) section 34 of the Adoption (Scotland) Act 1978**(j)** (removal of protected children from unsuitable surroundings), or

    (iii) article 35 of the Adoption (Northern Ireland) Order 1987**(k)** (removal of protected children from unsuitable surroundings);

(f) an order removing a child from his care has been made at any time under–

    (i) section 12 of the Foster Children Act 1980**(l)** or Part I of the Children Act 1958**(m)** (removal of foster children),

    (ii) section 12 of the Foster Children (Scotland) Act 1984**(n)** (removal of foster children), or

    (iii) section 8(1) of the Children and Young Persons Act (Northern Ireland) 1968 or section 6(1) of the Children and Young Persons Act (Northern Ireland) 1950 (removal of foster children);

(g) he has been convicted of any offence mentioned in the Schedule;

(h) he is a person who carried on, or was otherwise concerned with the management of, or had any financial interest in, a voluntary home which was removed from the register under

    (i) section 57(4) of the Child Care Act 1980**(o)**,

    (ii) paragraph 1(4) of Schedule 5 to the Act,

    (iii) section 99(4) of the Children and Young Persons Act (Northern Ireland) 1950, or

    (iv) section 127(4) of the Children and Young Persons Act (Northern Ireland) 1968;

(a) Section 12AA was inserted by paragraph 23 of Schedule 12 to the Children Act 1989.
(b) 1933 c.12.
(c) 1937 c.37.
(d) 1968 c.34 (N.I.).
(e) 1950 c.5 (N.I.).
(f) 1968 c.49.
(g) 1948 c.43.
(h) 1976 c.36. Section 34 of the Adoption Act 1976 was repealed on 14th October 1991 by Schedule 15 of the Children Act 1989 (Commencement and Transitional Provisions) Order 1991 (S.I. 1991/828).
(i) 1958 c.5; this was repealed by the Adoption Act 1976.
(j) 1978 c.28.
(k) S.I. 1987/2203 (N.I. 22).
(l) 1980 c.6.
(m) 1958 c.65; this was repealed by the Foster Children Act 1980.
(n) 1984 c.56.
(o) 1980 c.5. Section 57(4) was amended by section 11 of and paragraph 39 of Schedule 4, Part II to the Health and Social Services and Social Security Adjudications Act 1983.

(i) there has been a refusal to register a voluntary home in relation to an application made by him under–

    (i) section 57(3) of the Child Care Act 1980**(a)**,

    (ii) paragraph 1(2) of Schedule 5 to the Act,

    (iii) paragraph 5 of Schedule 5 to the Act,

    (iv) section 99(3) of the Children and Young Persons Act (Northern Ireland) 1950, or

    (v) section 127(3) of the Children and Young Persons Act (Northern Ireland) 1968;

(j) there has been a refusal to register a registered children's home in relation to an application made by him under paragraph 1 of Schedule 6 to the Act (application for registration);

(k) he is a person who carried on or was otherwise concerned with the management of or had any financial interest in a registered children's home and that home was removed from the register under paragraph 4 of Schedule 6 to the Act (cancellation of registration);

(l) he is a person in respect of whom a prohibition has been imposed under–

    (i) section 69 of the Act (power to prohibit private fostering),

    (ii) section 10 of the Foster Children Act 1980 or Part I of the Children Act 1958 (power to prohibit private fostering), or

    (iii) section 10 of the Foster Children (Scotland) Act 1984, or a notice in writing is given by a Health and Social Services Board under section 1(3) of the Children and Young Persons Act (Northern Ireland) 1968**(b)** (withholding consent to the care and maintenance of the child being undertaken by a person);

(m) he has at any time been refused registration in respect of nurseries day care or child minding or had any such registration cancelled under–

    (i) section 1 of the Nurseries and Child-Minders Regulation Act 1948**(c)**,

    (ii) section 5 of the Nurseries and Child-Minders Regulation Act 1948,

    (iii) Part X of the Act,

    (iv) section 11(5) of the Children and Young Persons Act (Northern Ireland) 1968, or

    (v) section 15 of the Children and Young Persons Act (Northern Ireland) 1968.

(n) he has at any time been refused registration or had such registration cancelled under section 62 of the Social Work (Scotland) Act 1968**(d)** (registration of establishments).

Disqualification in relation to voluntary homes

3.—(1) A person who is disqualified under section 68 of the Act from fostering a child privately shall not carry on, or be otherwise concerned in the management of, or have any financial interest in, a voluntary home unless he has–

    (a) disclosed to the Secretary of State the fact that he is so disqualified; and

    (b) obtained his written consent.

(2) No person shall employ a person who is so disqualified in a voluntary home unless he has–

    (a) disclosed to the Secretary of State the fact that that person is so disqualified; and

    (b) obtained the written consent of the Secretary of State.

(3) Where the Secretary of State refuses to give his consent under this regulation he shall inform the person carrying on or intending to carry on the voluntary home by a written notice which states–

(a) Section 57(3) was amended by section 11 of and paragraph 39 of Schedule 4, Part II to the Health and Social Services and Social Security Adjudications Act 1983 (c.41).

(b) Section 1(3) was amended by Schedule 16 to the Health and Personal Social Services (Northern Ireland) Order 1972 (S.I. 1972/1265 (N.I. 14)).

(c) 1948 c.53. Section 1 was amended by section 60 of the Health Services and Public Health Act 1968 (c.46).

(d) Section 62 was amended by section 3 of the Registered Establishments (Scotland) Act 1987 (c.40).

(a) the reason for the refusal;

(b) the right to appeal against the refusal to a Registered Homes Tribunal under paragraph 5 of Schedule 5 to the Act; and

(c) the time within which he may do so.

(4) Any person who contravenes paragraph (1) or (2) of this regulation shall be guilty of an offence and liable on summary conviction to imprisonment for a term not exceeding 6 months or to a fine not exceeding level 5 on the standard scale, or to both.

Signed by authority of the Secretary of State for Health.

Virginia Bottomley
Minister of State,
Department of Health

16th September 1991

Michael Forsyth
Minister of State,
Scottish Office

17th September 1991

SCHEDULE (regulation 2(g))

OFFENCES WHICH DISQUALIFY PERSONS FROM PRIVATE FOSTERING AND REGISTERING UNDER SECTION 71 OF THE ACT

1. Offences specified in Schedule 1 to the Children and Young Persons Act 1933**(a)** and Schedule 1 to the Criminal Procedure (Scotland) Act 1975**(b)** and Schedule 1 to the Children and Young Persons Act (Northern Ireland) 1968**(c)** and the Homosexual Offences (Northern Ireland) Order 1982**(d)**.

2. Any offence involving injury or threat of injury to another person.

3. Offences under any of the following–

(a) section 36(1)(b) or (c) of the Adoption Act 1976**(e)**, or section 36(1)(b) or (c) of the Adoption (Scotland) Act 1978**(f)**, or Article 37(1)(b) or (c) of the Adoption (Northern Ireland) Order 1987 (refusing to allow the visiting of a protected child or inspection of the premises or refusing to comply with or obstructing the removal of the child);

(b) sections 44(15), 49 or 50(9) of the Children Act 1989 or sections 17(8) or 71 of the Social Work (Scotland) Act 1968 or sections 6 to 10 of the Child Abduction Act 1984**(g)** or sections 9(1)(e) and (f), 32(3), 140(6) and 144(3) of the Children and Young Persons Act (Northern Ireland) 1968; section 32(3) of the Children and Young Persons Act 1969 (offences of intentional obstruction of a person executing an emergency protection order or in Scotland and Northern Ireland a place of safety order, or abduction or obstruction of lawful recovery of an abducted child);

(a) Schedule 1 has been amended by sections 48 and 51 of and Schedules 3 and 4 to the Sexual Offences Act 1956 (c.69), section 1(5) of the Protection of Children Act 1978 (c.37) as supplemented by section 160 of the Criminal Justice Act 1988 (c.33) and further amended by section 170 of and paragraphs 8 and 9 of Schedule 15 to that Act and Schedule 16 to that Act.

(b) Schedule 1 has been amended by section 21 of and Schedules 1 and 2 to the Sexual Offences (Scotland) Act 1976 (c.67) and section 170 of and paragraphs 50 and 51 of Schedule 15 to the Criminal Justice Act 1988.

(c) Schedule 1 has been amended by the Criminal Justice (Northern Ireland) Order 1980 (S.I. 1980/704 (N.I.16)); the Child Abduction (Northern Ireland) Order 1985 (S.I. 1985/1638 (N.I. 17)); the Mental Health (Northern Ireland) Order 1986 (S.I. 1986/595 (N.I. 4)). Reference in the Protection of Children (Northern Ireland) Order 1978 (S.I. 1978/104 (N.I. 17)) to offences under Schedule 1 include an offence under the Protection of Children (Northern Ireland) Order 1978.

(d) S.I. 1982/1536 (N.I. 19).

(e) Section 36(1)(c) of the Adoption Act 1976 was repealed on 14 October 1991 by Schedule 15 of the Children Act 1989 (Commencement and Transitional Provisions) Order 1991 (S.I. 1991/828).

(f) 1978 c.28.

(g) There is no exact equivalent to these provisions in Scotland; thus offences relating to children in places of safety, residential establishments or under control are dealt with by section 71 of the Social Work (Scotland) Act 1968 in so far as they relate to inducing/assisting abscondment and harbouring a child. Abduction of a child in care is dealt with under section 17(8) of the 1968 Act and abduction generally under Part II of the Child Abduction Act 1984 (c.37) which, in Scotland, is not an offence for the purposes of Schedule 1 to the Criminal Procedure (Scotland) Act 1975 (c.21).

(c) section 78 of the Act or section 14 of the Children and Young Persons Act (Northern Ireland) 1968**(a)** (providing day care or acting as a child minder in unregistered premises or contravening an enforcement order served on him by a local authority acting under that section);

(d) section 63(10) of the Act (caring for and accommodating a child in a children's home which is not registered) or paragraph 2(3) of Schedule 6 to the Act (breach of conditions attaching to registration of registered children's home);

(e) section 14 of the Children Act 1958, section 16 of the Foster Children Act 1980, section 70 of the Act, section 15 of the Foster Children (Scotland) Act 1984, or section 9(1) of the Children and Young Persons Act (Northern Ireland) 1968, or section 2(8) of the Children and Young Persons Act (Northern Ireland) 1950 (offences in respect of private fostering);

(f) section 29(5) of the Children Act 1948, section 57(5) of the Child Care Act 1980**(b)**, paragraph 1(5) of Schedule 5 to the Act, or sections 99(5) and 101(3) of the Children and Young Persons Act (Northern Ireland) 1950, or section 127(5) or 129(3) of the Children and Young Persons Act (Northern Ireland) 1968 (carrying on a voluntary home without it being registered or in contravention of a condition attached to registration);

(g) section 6(5), 60(3), 61, 62 or 68(3) of the Social Work (Scotland) Act 1968 (refusal of registration and offences in respect of day care or residential care);

(h) the common law offence in Scotland of plagium (theft of a child below the age of puberty);

(i) section 52(1)(a) or section 52(A) of the Civil Government (Scotland) Act 1982**(c)** (offences relating to indecent photographer of children).

EXPLANATORY NOTE

(This note is not part of the Regulations)

These Regulations replace the disqualifications contained in the Nurseries and Childminders Regulation Act 1948, the Child Care Act 1980 and the Foster Children Act 1980 which are repealed by the Children Act 1989. The Regulations also include the disqualifications contained in the Children's Homes Act 1982 (c.20) which had not been brought into force and are repealed by the 1989 Act. To the extent that they apply to disqualification from registration for childminding and day care the Regulations extend also to Scotland.

Regulation 2 and the Schedule specify various circumstances in which a person
– is disqualified from fostering a child privately;
– is disqualified from being registered as a childminder on domestic premises or as a person who provides day care for children under 8 on non-domestic premises; and
Regulation 3 provides that a person who is disqualified under section 68 of the Act from fostering a child privately shall not carry on or be involved with a voluntary children's home or employed in such an establishment without the consent of the Secretary of State.

By virtue of section 65 of the Children Act 1989 a person who is disqualified from fostering a child privately is also disqualified from carrying on or being concerned in the management of a children's home or be employed in such an establishment without the consent of the local authority.

Unlike the preceding legislation which related only to a specific activity, a disqualification under these provisions will serve also to disqualify a person from any of the activities specified in these Regulations.

(a) There is no provision for enforcement orders under the relevant Northern Ireland legislation.
(b) Section 57 was amended by section 11 of and paragraph 39 of Schedule 4 Part II to the Health and Social Services and Social Security Adjudications Act 1983.
(c) 1982 c.45. Section 52A was inserted by section 161 of the Criminal Justice Act 1988.

STATUTORY INSTRUMENTS

1991 No. 1689

CHILDREN AND YOUNG PERSONS

Child Minding and Day Care (Applications for Registration) Regulations 1991

Made - - - -	*23rd July 1991*
Laid before Parliament	*31st July 1991*
Coming into force	*14th October 1991*

The Secretary of State for Health in relation to England and Wales and the Secretary of State for Scotland in relation to Scotland in exercise of the powers conferred by paragraph 1(1) of Schedule 9 to the Children Act 1989**(a)**, and all other powers enabling them in that behalf, hereby makes the following Regulations:–

Citation and commencement

1. These Regulations may be cited as the Child Minding and Day Care (Applications for Registration) Regulations 1991, and shall come into force on 14th October 1991.

Interpretation

2. In these Regulations unless the context otherwise requires–

"the Act" means the Children Act 1989;

"full day care" means day care provided for children under the age of eight for a full working day in premises other than domestic premises;

"person in charge" means in relation to day care where the applicant is not an individual, the person appointed as the person in charge of providing the actual day care by the applicant;

"sessional day care" means day care provided for children under the age of eight for less than a full working day in premises other than domestic premises;

Applications for registration

3.—(1) The statement which, in accordance with paragraph 1(1)(a) of Schedule 9 to the Act, is to be contained in an application for registration under section 71 of the Act (statement with respect to the applicant), shall include the information specified in Schedule 1 to these Regulations.

(2) The statement which, in accordance with paragraph 1(1)(b) of Schedule 9 to the Act, is to be contained in an application for registration under section 71 of the Act (statement with respect to certain other persons), shall include the information specified in Schedule 2 to these Regulations.

(a) 1989 c. 41.

[NOTE: Please refer to SI 1991 No 2129 in this Annex which amends part of these Regulations.]

Signed by the authority of the Secretary of State for Health.

23rd July 1991

Virginia Bottomley
Minister of State,
Department of Health

Signed by the authority of the Secretary of State for Scotland.

23rd July 1991

Michael B. Forsyth
Minister of State,
Scottish Office

SCHEDULE 1 Regulation 3(1)

Information to be provided about the applicant

1. The full name of the applicant, including (if different) name at birth and any other former names, or where day care is to be provided by a partnership, committee or corporate or unincorporate body, the full names of the partners, members of the Committee, Board of Directors, or the Board, identifying the Chairman, Secretary and Treasurer, and the person in charge.

2. The address at which the children are to be looked after, and the applicant's and person in charge's address if different.

3. Whether the premises at which the children are to be looked after are domestic premises.

4. In the case of day care, a description of the facilities available to the applicant for day care, including the number of rooms, their functions, the numbers of lavatories and washbasins, any separate facilities for adult workers and access to the premises for cars.

5. Whether the applicant wishes to register as a child minder, or as a provider of day care, and if the latter whether he will provide full day care or sessional day care.

6. In the case of day care, the proposed hours for which the applicant wishes to provide day care.

7. Relevant experience of the applicant, and any person in charge, including any previous work with children or with elderly or disabled people, whether paid or not.

8. The number and ages of any children of the applicant or the person in charge or any children for whom either is to be responsible.

9. Any relevant qualifications (with dates) of the applicant or the person in charge giving details of the organisation running the course, the subjects studied the length of course and the name of the qualification.

10. The names of two referees for the applicant or the person in charge who may be contacted.

11. The name and address of the applicant's or the person in charge's general medical practitioner and whether he may be approached for details concerning the state of health of the applicant or person in charge, together with details of anything for which he is currently being treated by his general medical practitioner or by a hospital, and details of any hospital admissions during the last 2 years and of any serious illnesses in the last 5 years.

12. Details of any criminal convictions of the applicant or the person in charge, including–
  (a) the date of offence,
  (b) the nature of offence,

    (c) the place where it occurred,

    (d) the name of the court which gave the conviction,

    (e) the penalty imposed.

SCHEDULE 2

Regulation 3(2)

Information to be provided about any person assisting or likely to assist, or living or likely to live in the premises

1. In the case of child minders, names and date of birth of anyone living (or likely to be living) in the premises in which they intend to look after children, including members of the family and lodgers, and the name and address of any other person assisting (or likely to be assisting) in looking after the children.

2. In the case of day care applicants, names and dates of birth of anyone living (or likely to be living) on the premises to be used for day care, details of how many staff will be employed in looking after the children and in what capacity, details of any person in charge, any other person assisting (or likely to be assisting) in looking after children on the premises in question, with their name and address.

3. Details of any criminal convictions of any of the persons mentioned in paragraphs 1 or 2, including–

    (a) the date of offence,

    (b) the nature of offence,

    (c) the place where it occurred,

    (d) the name of the court which gave the conviction,

    (e) the penalty imposed.

EXPLANATORY NOTE

(This note is not part of the Regulations)

These Regulations require that child minders and providers of day care provide the information specified in Schedules 1 and 2 when applying for registration under the Children Act 1989.

The information required by Schedule 1 includes details about the applicant and where appropriate the person whom it is proposed will be in charge, including his qualification and experience, the premises in which the children will be looked after. Schedule 2 requires details of any other person living in, (or likely to be in,) those premises, and any person assisting (or likely to be assisting) in looking after the children.

£1.00 net

ISBN 0 11 014689 1

Printed in the United Kingdom for HMSO
879   WO1449   C51   7/91   452   7102   O/N 134937

1991 No. 2076

CHILDREN AND YOUNG PERSONS

The Child Minding and Day Care (Registration and Inspection Fees) Regulations 1991

Made - - - -	*11th September 1991*
Laid before Parliament	*17th September 1991*
Coming into force -	*14th October 1991*

The Secretary of State for Health in relation to England and Wales and the Secretary of State for Scotland in relation to Scotland in exercise of the powers conferred by sections 71(16) and 104(4) of, and paragraphs 1(3), 6(4) and 7 of Schedule 9 to the Children Act 1989**(a)**, and of all other powers enabling them in that behalf, hereby make the following Regulations:–

Citation and Commencement

1. These Regulations may be cited as the Child Minding and Day Care (Registration and Inspection Fees) Regulations 1991 and shall come into force on 14th October 1991.

Interpretation

2. In these Regulations unless the context otherwise requires–

"the Act" means the Children Act 1989;

"the 1948 Act" means the Nurseries and Child-Minders Regulation Act 1948**(b)**;

"full day care" means day care provided for children under the age of eight for a full working day on premises other than domestic premises;

"sessional day care" means day care provided for children under the age of eight for less than a full working day on premises other than domestic premises.

Registration

3.—(1) An application under section 71(1)(a) of the Act for registration as a child minder shall be accompanied by a fee of £10.00.

(2) An application under section 71(1)(b) for registration as a provider of day care shall be accompanied–

(a) where the applicant provides or is to provide full day care, by a fee of £100.00;

(b) where the applicant provides or is to provide sessional day care and does not provide and is not to provide full day care, by a fee of £10.00.

(3) Where immediately before the commencement of Part X of the Act either–

(a) any premises were registered under section 1(1)(a) of the 1948 Act, and a person applies within 12 months of the commencement of Part X to be registered under section 71 of the Act in respect of the provision of day care on those premises, or

---

(a) 1989 c.41.
(b) 1948 c.53.

[NOTE: Please refer to SI 1991 No 2129 in this Annex which amends part of these Regulations.]

(b) a person was registered under section 1(1)(b) of the 1948 Act (registration of nurseries and childminders) and that person applies under section 71 of the Act within 12 months of the commencement of Part X to be registered as a child minder,

no fee shall be payable.

Fee on Annual Inspection

4. The following fees are prescribed for the purposes of paragraph 7 of Schedule 9 to the Act (fees for annual inspection)–
  (a) where the person registered under section 71 of the Act is a child minder, the sum of £7.50;
  (b) where the person registered under section 71 of the Act is a provider of full day care, whether or not he is also a provider of sessional day care, the sum of £75.00;
  (c) where the person registered under section 71 of the Act is a provider of sessional day care and is not also a provider of full day care, the sum of £7.50.

Fee payable for issue of copy certificate

5. A fee of £5.00 is prescribed for the purposes of paragraph 6(4) of Schedule 9 to the Act (issue of copy certificate of registration under section 71 of the Act where certificate been lost or destroyed).

Signed by authority of the Secretary of State for Health.

Virginia Bottomley
Minister of State,
9th September 1991   Department of Health

Signed by authority of the Secretary of State for Scotland.

M. D. Forsyth
Minister of State,
11th September 1991   Scottish Office

EXPLANATORY NOTE

(This note is not part of the regulations)

These regulations provide for the fees that shall be paid to local authorities in relation to Part X of the Children Act 1989 (child minding and day care for young children).

Regulation 3 provides for the fees that shall accompany applications under section 71 of the 1989 Act (registration for child minding and day care) for registration as a child minder or provider of day care for children under eight.

Regulation 4 prescribes the fees that shall be payable in respect of the annual inspection of the premises of registered persons. Regulation 5 prescribes the fee that shall be payable where it is necessary to replace a lost certificate.

60p net

ISBN 0 11 015076 7

Printed in the United Kingdom for HMSO

879   WO1795   C40   9/91   452/3   4235   134976   913660

This Statutory Instrument is made to correct errors in S.I. 1991/1689 and 1991/2076 and is being issued free of charge to all known recipients of those Statutory Instruments

STATUTORY INSTRUMENTS

1991 No. 2129

CHILDREN AND YOUNG PERSONS

The Child Minding and Day Care (Applications for Registration and Registration and Inspection Fees) (Amendment) Regulations 1991

Made - - - -	*22nd September 1991*
Laid before Parliament	*23rd September 1991*
Coming into force -	*14th October 1991*

The Secretary of State for Health in relation to England and Wales and the Secretary of State for Scotland in relation to Scotland in exercise of the powers conferred by sections 71(16) and 104(4) of and paragraphs 1(1) and (3), 6(4) and 7 of Schedule 9 to the Children Act 1989**(a)** and of all other powers enabling them in that behalf hereby make the following Regulations:–

Citation and commencement

1. These Regulations may be cited as the Child Minding and Day Care (Applications for Registration and Registration and Inspection Fees) (Amendment) Regulations 1991 and shall come into force on 14th October 1991 immediately after the Child Minding and Day Care (Applications for Registration) Regulations 1991**(b)** and the Child Minding and Day Care (Registration and Inspection Fees) Regulations 1991**(c)**.

Amendment to the Child Minding and Day Care (Applications for Registration) Regulations 1991

2. Regulation 2 of the Child Minding and Day Care (Applications for Registration) Regulations 1991 shall be amended as follows–

    (a) in the definition of "full day care" for the words "a full working day" there shall be substituted the words "a continuous period of four hours or more in any day";

    (b) in the definition of "sessional day care" for the words "a full working day" there shall be substituted the words "a continuous period of four hours in any day".

Amendment to the Child Minding and Day Care (Registration and Inspection Fees) Regulations 1991

3. Regulation 2 of the Child Minding and Day Care (Registration and Inspection Fees) Regulations 1991 shall be amended as follows–

    (a) in the definition of "full day care" for the words "a full working day" there shall

---

(a) 1989 c.41.
(b) S.I. 1991/1689.
(c) S.I. 1991/2076.

be substituted the words "a continuous period of four hours or more in any day";

(b) in the definition of "sessional day care" for the words "a full working day" there shall be substituted the words "a continuous period of four hours in any day".

Signed by the authority of the Secretary of State for Health

22nd September 1991

Virginia Bottomley.
Minister of State, Department of Health

Signed by the authority of the Secretary of State for Scotland

22nd September 1991

Michael Forsyth.
Minister of State, Scottish Office

EXPLANATORY NOTE

(This note is not part of the Regulations)

These Regulations amend the definition of "full day care" and "sessional day care" in the Child Minding and Day Care (Applications for Registration) Regulations 1991 and the Child Minding and Day Care (Registration and Inspection Fees) Regulations 1991.

60p net

ISBN 0 11 015129 1

Printed in the United Kingdom for HMSO

879   WO1839   C40   9/91   452/3   4235   134976   913858

Printed in the United Kingdom for HMSO.
Dd.295241, 10/91, C280, 3385/4, 5673, 169541.